Uncovering Your Ancestry Through Family Photographs

Uncovering Your Ancestry through Family Photographs

Maureen A. Taylor

BETTERWAY BOOKS
CINCINNATI, OHIO
www.familytreemagazine.com

About the Author

Maureen A. Taylor, a genealogist and photo-historian, has written three books on genealogy, including *Through the Eyes of Your Ancestors*. She has written articles for the *Daguerrian Annual, The New England And Genealogical Register, Rhode Island History, Rhode Island Roots* and the *Computer Genealogist*. Taylor lectures on photography and genealogy at conferences around the country.

Uncovering Your Ancestry Through Family Photographs. Copyright © 2000 by Maureen A. Taylor. Manufactured in the United States of America. All rights reserved. No part of this book may be reproduced in any form or by any electronic or mechanical means including information storage and retrieval systems without permission in writing from the publisher, except by a reviewer, who may quote brief passages in a review. Published by Betterway Books, an imprint of F&W Publications, Inc., 1507 Dana Avenue, Cincinnati, Ohio 45207. (800) 289-0963. First edition.

Other fine Betterway Books are available from your local bookstore or direct from the publisher.

04 03 02 01 00   5 4 3 2 1

Library of Congress Cataloging-in-Publication Data

Taylor, Maureen A.
    Uncovering your ancestry through family photographs / by Maureen A. Taylor.—1st ed.
      p.   cm.
    Includes index.
    ISBN 1-55870-527-9 (alk. paper)
    1. Genealogy—Handbooks, manuals, etc. 2. Portrait photography—History. I. Title.
CS14.T39   2000
929'.1'072—dc21   99-051778

Editor: Cindy Laufenberg
Production editor: Christine Doyle
Interior designer: Sandy Kent
Cover designer: Matthew Gaynor

To my parents

Acknowledgments

There are so many people to thank for their encouragement and support when I was writing this book. My friends Jane Schwerdtfeger and Lynn Betlock listened to ideas. Several friends and colleagues read the manuscript and offered suggestions: Marcia Melnyk; David Mishkin of Just Black & White; Nancy Rexford; Alison Cywin; and Jonathan Galli, CG. Other individuals acted as consultants on research problems, in particular Chris Steele of the Massachusetts Historical Society and Jerome Anderson of the New England Historic Genealogical Society.

I am very grateful to Sharon DeBartolo Carmack for introducing me to Betterway. Without her prodding, this book would not be a reality.

I especially need to thank my husband, Dexter, for his patient reading of the manuscript. My efforts are always directed to children. Hopefully my own, James and Sarah, will come to love history as much as I do.

Icons Used in This Book

 Brick Wall Buster — How to turn dead ends into opportunities

 Case Study — Examples of this book's advice at work

 CD Source — Databases and other information available on CD-ROM

 Definitions — \di'fin\ vb — Terminology and jargon explained

 For More Info — Where to turn for more in-depth coverage

 Idea Generator — Techniques and prods for further thinking

 Important — Information and tips you can't overlook

 Internet Source — Where on the web to find what you need

 Library/Archive Source — Repositories that might have the information you need

 Microfilm Source — Information available on microfilm

 Money Saver — Getting the most out of research dollars

 Notes — Thoughts, ideas and related insights

 Printed Source — Directories, books, pamphlets and other paper archives

 Quotes — Useful words direct from the experts

 Reminder — "Don't-Forget" items to keep in mind

 Research Tip — Ways to make research more efficient

 See Also — Where in this book to find related information

 Sources — Where to go for information, supplies, etc.

 Step By Step — Walkthroughs of important procedures

 Supplies — Advice on day-to-day office tools

 Technique — How to conduct research, solve problems, and get answers

 Timesaver — Shaving minutes and hours off the clock

 Tip — Ways to make research more efficient

 Warning — Stop before you make a mistake

Table of Contents At a Glance

Table of Contents

Introduction

"The likeness is called a good one, I believe, though, if the family proverb be true, it must be a very ugly picture. My claim to pre-eminent 'homeliness' has never been disputed."

—Letter from Isaac Newton Cushman to Henry Wyles Cushman, 1854. From the Cushman Collection, New England Historic Genealogical Society

Our ancestors stare at us from faded photographs, captured for eternity by a camera. The images, however, offer only clues to their identity and personality. In some cases, a handwritten scrawl may appear on the back of the image identifying the person only as "Aunt Sally." As genealogists we attempt to assemble our family story by trying to place a face with an actual name.

On winter afternoons, my sister and I would sit with our mother and talk about the last fifty years of our family history, using photographs as the inspiration for the stories. I would spend hours imagining what life was really like for the people in the pictures. I would search their faces for recognizable resemblances. Whom did my sister resemble? Was it true that almost everyone had blue eyes? The images never changed, but as we grew older our questions became more sophisticated and the stories became more involved. No matter how hard we tried, the images always retained secrets that could never be divulged. Why was a particular dress selected for a portrait? Why was the photo taken in that location? Why were certain people included or excluded?

Often we accept photographs at face value. As genealogists, however, we know that there is a wealth of information waiting to be uncovered in the family photo album. Who is depicted and who is not? What do their clothes tell us? Where are they posed and with whom? Examining these images will initially raise more questions than answers.

You can construct lists of questions about family photographs. If the photograph was a formal portrait you may ask, Why did they choose those props? Did relatives change their appearance for the photographer? Did he or she adopt a new hairstyle, or remove a pair of glasses? What emotions are

Who's the photographer in your family? *David Lambert*

present? Does the pose and expression tell anything about the individual? If you look closely you raise questions whose answers shed light on the life, times and personalities of your ancestors.

WHAT IS A FAMILY PHOTOGRAPH COLLECTION?

A family photograph collection is more than a random collection of images; it is a time capsule of the lives of our ancestors. In the boxes of photos there may be formal portraits, as well as snapshots of vacations, relatives gathered for special events, friends and pets. You will learn about what was important to your ancestors. Each individual image is full of information, but a collection of photographs, once arranged and identified, can tell a story of a lifetime. The images are documentation of ancestral lives and interests. They provide clues for further genealogical research or furnish material not found in any standard genealogical resource. The images however only tell part of the story. In order to research ancestors one has to look at all the documents created in their lifetime. Only then will you have a complete "picture" of your ancestors. When visual and written materials are combined in a family history, a wonderful story emerges.

Think about the moments you immortalize with your camera. It is difficult to find a household today without a camera, yet to our ancestors picture taking was a new endeavor. Photography changed the way our ancestors thought about themselves and the world. The family photo collection became a valuable possession. It contained a record of the past. Pictures of the deceased members and family milestones could be reviewed and used to inform the newer members of the family. The content of each family collection is unique.

When you gather all your family photographs together from their various storage places, you may be surprised by the diversity. If your family collection dates from the beginning of photography (1839-40), you may have a wide variety of photographic examples. The pictorial documentation of ancestral lives is vast. Spread out a group of the images and study the panorama of a family's visual history. It forms a timeline. You can watch a baby grow to old age as the photographic process changes. It is a history of the births, loves and deaths of our ancestors.

Studio portraits of immaculately dressed and posed family members allow us to view our ancestors with a certain distance, while snapshots involve us in their lives. Snapshots provide us with an opportunity to see our ancestors

Photographs provide genealogists with visual clues about the lives of their ancestors.
Collection of the author

at play, at work or in their homes. By researching family photographs, you will gain a better understanding of the lives of your ancestors.

A close friend of mine lost everything she owned in a fire. This caused me to reflect on what I would save if given an opportunity. After making sure that all the members of my family were safe, I would grab my small collection of photographs. That is my family memory. My children's first steps, riding without training wheels, and birthday parties. It is also the only record in my possession of my grandparents. The only grandparent I ever knew lives in those pictures and connects me with the past.

ABOUT THIS BOOK

For many individuals, the anonymous faces that stare back from shoe boxes and albums tucked away in the attic or closet are interesting but puzzling. This book enables you to discover the visual heritage of your family by evaluating and understanding the various aspects of the photographs in your possession. It will assist you in your quest to find out more about your relatives by explaining how to identify the type of photo, research the photographer and date the costume. You will learn how to compare images for facial characteristics. Other sections help you build a family photograph collection and learn the research techniques unique to photo research. Each chapter contains charts and illustrations to guide you through the process. Case studies provide examples of how other people have solved family photographic mysteries.

The photographs that appear in this book were selected on the basis of their visual value. The majority were purchased for use in this publication and lack identification. The sight of all of these unidentified images for sale at auctions has inspired me to write this book. Our family photographs are too valuable to become someone else's "instant ancestors."

Any images used in the case studies are primarily from the collections of friends and family and have been identified using the techniques described in this book.

HOW TO USE IT

The purpose of this book is to assist you with the identification and interpretation of your family images.

- Use it as a reference tool (bibliographies, charts and worksheets).
- Understand the process of photo identification.
- Learn how to locate additional family photographs and build a collection.
- Expand your skills to include the resources particular to photo research.

ONE

Bringing the Past to Life

"I think this was Nathaniel Cutton's sister. We always called her Aunt Margaret."

—Anonymous from the back of a photograph

W hen was the last time you looked at your family photographs? If you haven't taken them out of their storage place recently, now is the time. **One of the first steps in compiling a genealogy is to examine possible sources of information in your home.** Your photographs are a valuable resource for family historians.

Genealogy and photography are linked in a family photograph collection. Family history is about the individuals in the photographs. The pictures more than any other document can bring the past to life. They provide insights into the lives of our ancestors. Photographs show you who attended weddings, birthday celebrations and other important family events. They may provide you with a sense of an ancestor's personality. Every photograph of Uncle Charlie may show him clowning for the camera while Aunt Minnie smiles demurely.

Photographs can even unite families. Genealogists in the same family may share research unaware that their photo collections contain copies of the same images. The unidentified images in your collection may be identified in a relative's collection. You may have an unidentified photograph of a young child, while a distant relative has several identified photographs of that same individual at different ages.

Important

COMPILING A VISUAL HISTORY

As genealogists, it is important for us to compile the visual history of our families as well as the written information. Each image contains a series of clues that will assist you with your research. A photographer's imprint may enlighten you as to the place of immigration, or an artifact depicted in an image may be the same item you own today. By closely examining a picture

Reminder

you may see a chair that matches one in your house. The photograph gives you a clue to the previous owner of the object.

Costume can reveal information about the ethnic origins of your family. You may have images in your collection that show ancestors dressed in attire from a particular country. You may even discover a female ancestor's political viewpoint through an image; early women reformers adapted a certain style of dress that included pants. Such information in the photographs will provide numerous clues about your family.

Our ancestors often sat for multiple portraits. *David Lambert*

Photographs can help you re-create your ancestor's lives. Documents can provide data, but only pictures can provide a framework for that information.

As genealogists we are trying to solve family mysteries. Photographs raise questions about your family. Why was grandfather wearing that costume? Where are all the children in the group photograph? Using your skills as a genealogist, you may be able to answer those questions and bring new meaning to your family album.

Family photograph collections are as diverse as families themselves. The composition and size of a family photograph collection depends, in part, on the variables of interest, economics, place of settlement, access to a photographer or equipment and even religious affiliation. If a family lived in a rural area they would not necessarily have access to a photographer, so there may not be any photographs of them. Affluent families enjoyed photography as a leisure time activity, while urban working class families had little time to engage in such an activity. Some religions, such as the Quakers, originally discouraged members from having photographs taken. If your ancestors were part of a religious group that discouraged photography, your collection may not be very large. **When looking at the photographs in your possession, remember to think about your family in the context in which they lived.**

One of the contributing factors to the size of a family collection was the novelty of photography in the nineteenth century. For instance, in your collection you may find several different types of images of one ancestor taken around the same time. Photographers advertised the newest techniques and styles of photographs in terms of method, content or purpose to entice customers to return to their studios. Our ancestors, as consumers, sought the latest trend or new technique in order to capture the best representation of themselves.

Photographers lured customers into their studios by advertising new techniques and products. *New England Historic Genealogical Society*

Technological limitations, however, influenced the quantity and content of photos. For instance, all photographs in the early nineteenth century were taken under natural light, as artificial lighting wasn't available until the 1880s. The limits of the early equipment also influenced the type of image that could be taken. Acquiring a basic understanding of the photographic methods can provide background in your investigation of your family photographs.

Important

There are several stages involved in evaluating, dating and possibly identifying a photograph. Determining the method of photography, researching the photographer, appraising the costume, and verifying the genealogical information are important parts of the process. It will be necessary to consult experts and conduct library research. The process can be time-consuming, but very rewarding.

To get started, you must develop a new way of looking at photographs, as the smallest detail may yield an important clue or the answer to a family mystery. A family heirloom such as a piece of jewelry may enable you to identify a person in a photograph. A sign in the background, props and equipment may also help date an image. You will need to scrutinize each photograph closely to itemize all the particulars.

HOW TO GET STARTED

The first rule of family picture research is to be a good genealogist. It is necessary to develop a research strategy, keep good records, and try again if at first you don't succeed. A picture researcher/genealogist uses whatever resources will help solve the problem. By breaking the project down into steps, it is easier to piece together the history of an image and draw conclusions regarding the identity of the events, persons or family members depicted.

Steps in Family Photo Research:
1. Examine your family photographs.
2. Fill out a worksheet.
3. Develop a research plan.
4. Research the key elements of the picture.
5. Draw conclusions based on your research.
6. Look for other family photographs.

The first two steps are obviously related. **You examine the photograph and copy onto a worksheet the information that is known.** The blank spaces in the worksheet, like the one on page 9, will identify your research priorities.

It is also important to involve your relatives early in the identification process. Relatives may be able to identify some of the individuals in a group portrait or suggest a date for an event.

Key Elements in Dating Your Photographs:
1. Type of photography
2. Internal details (props, background, facial characteristics)
3. Photographer's name
4. Costume
5. Genealogical research

**USEFUL FORMS
YOU CAN REPRODUCE**

For a full-sized blank copy of worksheets see Appendix F, page 124. You are free to photocopy these forms for personal use.

WORKSHEET
Prints

Title/Subject/Caption
[Alice McDuff]
Identifying marks
Photographers Imprint on Lower Right
Photographer's name Jean L. Harbeck Pawtucket City Directories 1903-1940
Coloring details None
Costume description Fitted dress with large buttons wearing watch & locket
Other:

Owner's name	Maureen Taylor
Address	
Telephone number	
Condition	Excellent
Type of image	Photo Print
Size (Height × Width)	5" × 3½"
Mounted	No
Thickness	
Type of mount	None
Original or copy of print:	Original
Photographer's imprint	Harbeck-Pawtucket
Dates of operation	1903-1940
Props/background	Props—Bench, Bannister Background—painted backdrop with columns
Costume time frame	1910-1916
Whereabouts of negative	Unknown

An initial step is to try to determine the date of the image by the technique used to take the picture. Each method or style of photography has identifiable characteristics. By comparing the image in question to a chart of stylistic differences (see chapters two, three and four), you can determine a range of dates.

When you closely examine the image, details will become apparent. Props, backdrops and signage, for instance, can help identify when and where an image was taken. Facial characteristics can also assist in the identification process.

A group portrait contains many details to help you date an image. *Grant Emison*

See Also

Chapter 6, starting on page 44, for details on identifying photographers, and Chapter 8, starting on page 63, for details on identifying clothing and accessories.

If the photographer is identified by name, you will be able to determine when they were in business. This can help assign a specific date to an image as well as a location. These are important facts for your genealogical research.

The clothing worn by the people in the picture provides an additional layer of information. Identifying the style of clothing in an image is key to dating the photograph. Women's clothing, in particular, can be broken down into distinct features that can place an image within a time frame.

Genealogical research will provide you with materials to further identify the photograph. Family papers, census records and newspapers can place a photograph within a timeframe.

Ways to Date a Photograph

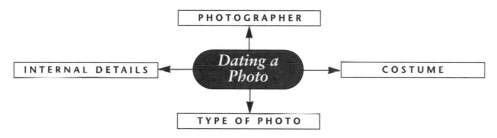

Library research will help you put all the pieces together. At some point only a library will have the resources you need to answer specific questions. Books, manuscripts and on-line resources can provide direction when you seem to run out of ideas.

One of the primary rules of genealogy is to cite your sources. Citations validate the information found and provide a reference point for further research. For each photo you should develop a worksheet that enables you to record your findings and citations. Carry the worksheets and *photocopies* of the images with you on research trips. Attaching a photocopy of the image to the worksheet will help you avoid damaging or losing the original.

Group portraits require a modification of the worksheet. **In addition to attaching a photocopy or slide to the worksheet, in the case of group portraits, a sketch of the photograph can provide a key to the image.** Each person in the image is assigned a number to help with identification as in

Reminder

Tip

Key to Group Portrait

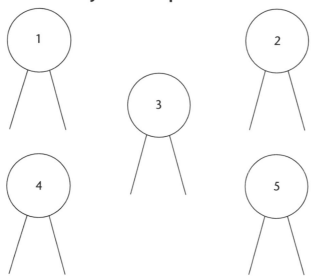

1. Ellen Derry Stone
2. Alberta Davis (1912–1996)
3.
4. Miss Meagher (school teacher)
5.
Include name and life dates for each known individual.

Warning

Supplies

TOOLS FOR EXAMINING AND HANDLING PHOTOGRAPHS

White cotton gloves
Loupe or magnifying glass
Measuring tape
Polypropylene sleeves

Important

the example on page 11. Examples of worksheets appear in Appendix F, pages 124–127.

There are a few basic tools that can assist with the investigative process. **You should always wear lint-free, white cotton gloves to prevent the oils from your hands from marring the surface of the image.** These can be purchased at any hardware store or are available from the suppliers listed in Appendix B, page 118. Fingerprint damage is not always immediately apparent. It may take time to appear. By using gloves you are preventing further damage to the photos from skin oils, dirt or moisture that may be present on your hands. You should wash the gloves after use to prevent transferring dirt from them to other images.

A magnifying glass can enlarge and illuminate details not readily apparent, such as the wording of a sign in the background. A photographer's loupe, a type of magnifying lens, is available at most photo stores and allows you to focus on a single feature at a time.

A measuring tape can be a helpful tool. One of the clues for identifying the type of image is its size. Card photographs, for instance, were available in a variety of dimensions.

When you are finished examining the image, it is helpful to place it in a special sleeve to protect it from future damage. Sleeves of archival material such as polypropylene can be purchased from conservation supply houses.

If your first attempts at research are unsuccessful, put the photograph aside and work on another. The information you find during research on another image may provide solutions to the first image.

In order to draw conclusions about the images you are researching, it is best to remember the basic rules of photo research.

A FEW RULES TO FOLLOW

1. Be a good genealogist.
2. Use care when handling photographs.
3. Use a worksheet.
4. Develop a research strategy.
5. Cite your sources.
6. Use all resources available to solve a photo mystery.

If you follow this advice, you should have a better understanding of the images in your collection: what type of photographs they are, an approximate date for each and in the best cases, you will have developed conclusions about the identity of the individuals in the photographs.

TWO

Cased Images: Daguerreotypes, Ambrotypes and Tintypes

"If our children and children's children to the third and fourth generation are not in possession of portraits of their ancestors, it will be no fault of the Daguerreotypists of the present day; for verily, they are limning faces at a rate that promises soon to make every man's home a Daguerrean Gallery. From little Bess, the baby, up to great-great-grandpa, all must now have their likenesses; and even the sober [Quaker], who heretofore rejected all the vacuities of portrait-taking, is tempted to sit in the operator's chair . . ."

—T.S. Arthur, "American Characteristics: The Daguerreotypist" *Godey's Lady's Book*, 38, May 1849

The very first photographs our ancestors saw amazed them. They marveled over the intricacy and minute detail of those earliest images. It is not possible for us living in a visually oriented world to imagine what it must have been like to see a photograph for the first time. Our ancestors embraced photography and fell in love with its qualities. The demand for the new images spurred inventors into developing new and cheaper ways to produce images.

The progression from the first photographs, called daguerreotypes, to the contemporary digital photograph is an interesting history. It is a topic genealogists need to understand in order to relate to their photograph collections. Identifying the type of photograph you are looking at is the first step in the process of evaluating and interpreting your family's photographic heritage. It is part of setting your family into the historical context in which they lived.

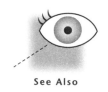

See Also

See Appendix A for a timeline of photographic history.

DAGUERREOTYPES

Definitions

If you have ever seen a small metal photograph with a reflective surface, then you have looked upon a daguerreotype. Our ancestors embraced this new technology which was invented by Frenchman Louis Daguerre in 1839. Daguerreotypes were more affordable than painted portraits but not as flattering. The clarity and truthfulness of the images awed our ancestors. Daguerreotypes became known as mirrors with a memory. A popular 1850s children's story, "Grandmother Lee's Portfolio," included the following quote from a grandmother who had just received some daguerreotypes from her grandchildren.

> I'm so happy! I keep them where I can look at them all the time, with the cases open, that your bright faces may be looking upon me constantly; and at night, when I go to bed, I stand them open on the table side of me, where they may be the first things I shall see, as I open my eyes in the morning.

A daguerreotype consists of an image, mat, cover glass and case.
Chris Steele/Massachusetts Historical Society.

The earliest daguerreotypes were still-life subjects because it took several minutes to create the image. However, once the exposure time decreased, the majority of daguerreotypes were portraits. They were presented in the same type of case used for painted miniature portraits. Over a period of years the daguerreotype eventually replaced the painted portrait in popularity.

DAGUERREOTYPE SIZES	
Imperial/Mammoth plate	Larger than 6½″ × 8½″
Whole Plate	6½″ × 8½″
Half Plate	4½″ × 5½″
Quarter Plate	3¼″ × 4¼″
Sixth Plate	2¾″ × 3¼″
Ninth Plate	2″ × 2½″

The major flaw of the new invention was that it required technical skill and artistic talent in order to capture a good image. Initially, the long exposure times made it difficult to take a complimentary portrait. Individuals look stiff and uncomfortable in daguerreotypes and they were. Subjects were asked not to smile because it was difficult to hold it for a long time. Imagine having to hold a particular pose for several minutes without moving.

Daguerreotypists also used implements and tricks to assure a good image. Head braces attached to chair backs helped individuals hold their head still for the required amount of time. Wax was used to fix ears that stuck out and cotton could be used to puff up hollow looking cheeks. The best images were those that were well lit and well composed.

Despite the quality issues, daguerreotypes were very popular. More than three million were produced in the United States by 1844. Within a year of the daguerreotype's invention, studios operated in all the major cities of the eastern United States and itinerants brought the medium to the smaller towns. Studios displayed sample portraits so prospective customers could judge the quality of their work. Studios in the larger cities had elaborate sitting rooms and furnishings. Comfortable surroundings allowed patrons to relax before having their picture taken.

A visit to the daguerreotypist studio required patience and preparation. Studios and popular magazines published guides on dressing for the camera.

For More Info

FOR FURTHER DISCUSSION

For more on this topic, see *Mirror Image: The Influences of the Daguerreotype on American Society*, by Richard Rudisill (Albuquerque: University of New Mexico Press, 1971).

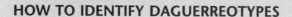

HOW TO IDENTIFY DAGUERREOTYPES

1. Shiny, reflective surface.

2. Must be held at a particular angle to see the image.

3. By tilting them at a different angle, the image will change from a negative to a positive.

4. Usually in a case although not always.

5. Sometimes colored or tinted.

6. Can be confused with cased ambrotypes and tintypes.

Tip

Godey's Lady's Book advised dressing in dark or patterned fabric that would not reflect too much light. White, pink or light blue were to be avoided, while lacework, or a scarf or shawl added to the picture. A dark vest and cravat were the recommended dress for men. Children dressed similar to adults in plaid or dark striped dresses. If a person showed up for a sitting without the necessary accoutrements, the studio would often supply props, shawls, lace collars and even jewelry to enhance the portrait.

Daguerreotypists came from a variety of occupational backgrounds. Some were painters, others sought a way to augment their regular livelihood. For instance G.G. Walker of Providence, Rhode Island, took daguerreotypes and sold musical instruments.

AMBROTYPES

It was not long before people became dissatisfied with the daguerreotype. It was expensive, difficult to view and required long sittings. In the mid-1850s a new type of image appeared, the ambrotype. **Where the daguerreotype used a metal surface, the ambrotype used glass. The image was formed by coating a piece of glass with collodion, a mixture of ether and guncotton.**

Each cased ambrotype portrait consisted of the glass image, a dark backing, a cover glass and edging. The metal edging, known as a preserver, held all the pieces together. Most ambrotypes were backed with either black velvet or paper. A coating of black varnish could also be used to save money. The black backing brings the portrait into focus. When the image is removed from its backing the detail of the image is lost to the viewer.

There are a few similarities between a daguerreotype and an ambrotype. Each image was a unique copy. Only a single ambrotype or daguerreotype could be produced at a time. If an individual wanted other copies of a

Definitions

Important

There are three parts to an ambrotype: the image, mat and preserver.
Chris Steele/Massachusetts Historical Society

portrait, additional photographs had to be taken. The images typically appear reversed in both ambrotypes and daguerreotypes. Details appear as they would in a mirror. Some photographers solved this by flipping over the ambrotype and facing the collodion side out.

By 1856 the ambrotype enjoyed a short-lived period of popularity. It was cheaper to produce and did not have to be viewed in a special light. While the daguerreotype required a certain amount of training to obtain a good impression, ambrotypists could easily learn how to capture an image.

Ambrotypes were available in the same sizes as the daguerreotypes since the same cases were used. The most popular sizes were the sixth and quarter plate.

TINTYPES

In 1856, an Ohio chemistry professor named Hamilton Smith patented the process of coating an iron plate with collodion. The iron was coated with a black or brown varnish. The resulting image was a direct positive when viewed on the dark background. These images were known as melainotypes or ferrotypes, because of the iron backing. **They were also called tintypes because of the use of tin shears to cut the photographs out of the iron sheet.**

\di'fin\ *vb*

Definitions

The iron tintypes were more durable and weighed less than daguerreotypes and ambrotypes. They did not scratch as easily as daguerreotypes or break like ambrotypes. Unlike the daguerreotype and the ambrotype, tintypes could be carried in a pocket or sent through the mail without risk. A coating of clear varnish further protected the image area.

Tintypes are photographs on iron plates.
Collection of the author

Most photographic improvements prior to the tintype had been developed in Europe. The tintype, however, is considered an American invention.

It was the only photographic format patented by an American. Tintypes remained in use from 1856 until the mid-1930s.

Tintypes were fast and cheap to produce. A customer could walk into a studio, sit for a portrait and walk out in as little as ten minutes with multiple copies. The speed with which a picture could be taken led the process to be referred to as "instantaneous." An image could cost as little as a few cents.

TINTYPE SIZES	
Whole plate	6½″ × 8½″
Half plate	4½″ × 5½″
Quarter plate	3½″ × 4½″
Sixth plate	2¾″ × 3¼″
Ninth plate	2″ × 2½″
Sixteenth plate	1⅝″ × 2⅛″
Gem or thumbnail	1″ × 1″ (or smaller)

These inexpensive images were commonly found on the frontier, in small towns and in working class urban districts. Individuals who were previously unable to afford a portrait could now obtain one. The images were acceptable, even though they had a cold, dull appearance and all the whites appeared gray.

The popularity of tintypes was also driven by new applications. The election of 1860 employed campaign buttons made of tintypes with presidential candidates on them. The Civil War also helped. Traveling photographers often accompanied military units and set up shop where they camped. The low cost of the image allowed even the poorest soldier access to an image he could send home to his family. In the twentieth century, vacationers would return home from resorts carrying tintypes.

At first only one image could be produced at a time, but once cameras with multiple lenses appeared, identical portraits could be produced in one sitting. Individuals could now obtain myriad copies of their portraits to give to friends and family. The number of lenses on the camera limited the number of copies produced.

Tintypes appeared in many of the same image sizes as the daguerreotypes and ambrotypes. The majority of tintypes were 6½″ × 8½″. The size of a sheet of iron and the type of camera limited the maximum size to 10″ × 14″. The smallest images were approximately an inch square. These tiny images were called "gems" or "thumbnails" because they were no larger than a person's thumb.

Since tintypes were approximately the same size as daguerreotypes and ambrotypes, photographers could place them in presentation cases. There were a few exceptions. Special photographic albums were developed to hold the smallest images. They fit in the palm of a hand. Since tintypes were so durable they could also be placed in paper mats.

Most of the tintypes produced are a brown or chocolate color. Collectors claim that tintypes were also manufactured in a variety of other colors including blue and yellow, but these are extremely rare.

HOW TO IDENTIFY A CASED IMAGE

The chart below describes the major characteristics of each type of image commonly found in cases. The most difficult to distinguish are the ambrotype and tintype because of the similarity of their appearance when in a case.

Sometimes some of the backing will be missing from an ambrotype and the negative qualities can be seen. In cases where this is not apparent, you can carefully remove an image from its case using a small suction cup or by gently prying the image from the case. **Be careful not to damage the case itself in the process.**

Daguerreotypes are easily identified because of their reflective surface. But you can still find misidentified images for sale by individuals not familiar with the differences.

Warning

CASED IMAGE CHARACTERISTICS		
Daguerreotype	**Ambrotype**	**Tintypes**
Mirror like surface	Negative on glass; appears as a positive image	Negative on iron; appears as a positive image
Must be held at an angle to be seen	Backed with a dark background	Fixed on a black metal background
Usually cased	Usually cased	Paper mat or case
1839	1854	1856

Handling Suggestions: *Don't Clean Them Yourself!*

Individuals with cased images in their collection are often tempted to clean a cased image themselves. This can irreparably damage the image. What looks like dirt on the glass could be a problem with the image itself. It is best to leave the restoration work to professional conservators. **There is a list of conservators in Appendix B page 103.**

A daguerreotype consists of several different layers—the metal plate, the mat, and the cover glass with an edging to hold the parts together—then finally it is placed in a case. These images are inherently fragile. The salts on the metal plate can be wiped away or the plate scratched, permanently obscuring or damaging the image.

Daguerreotypes will often exhibit a type of haze on the glass or a halo around the image. It is difficult for an untrained individual to ascertain the cause of the damage and how to prevent further deterioration.

There are two reasons why ambrotypes are fragile: they are made on glass and the image is a coating on the surface of the glass. Any attempt to

See Also

clean the surface will either damage or destroy your image. The collodion can, over time, lift away from the glass surface and flake off.

Tintypes or ferrotypes are somewhat more durable, but again the collodion is coated on a metal plate. When exposed to moisture the iron will rust and any type of surface abrasion will remove or scratch the image.

With these cautions in mind the best rule to follow is: *Leave all restoration to a professional.*

DATING A CASED IMAGE

Important

Because of the fragility of early photographs, they required a case. The four pieces of a standard cased image were the image, a cover glass, a mat and a preserver to hold the unit together. **The parts of the photograph that can be useful for dating purposes are the construction of the case, its surface design and the mat.** Case elements include the material of which it is made, the hinges and the design. Cases were made of wood, papier-mâché, leather or a hard substance that resembles plastic.

The basic construction of cases in the 1840s consisted of wood frames with embossed leather. The clasp was typically a hook and eye. Inside the case was a velvet pad. The velvet, which could be red, purple or green, could be embossed with the photographer's name and address.

Papier-mâché cases were also popular in the 1840s. They could be made waterproof with a variety of substances such as sulphate of iron, quicklime, glue or white of eggs. They could also be made fireproof with borax and phosphate of soda. The decorative features of the cases were enhanced with inlaid mother-of-pearl.

In 1852, Samuel Peck patented a new, more durable case. In some publications authors mistakenly refer to these "union cases" as being composed of gutta-percha, an early plastic. Actually composed of gum shellac, woody fibers or other fibrous material, the new cases had several advantages. They could be molded to hold any surface design, dyed, and were available in a variety of shapes. Most of the cases remaining today are black or brown, but they were also manufactured in red, green, tan and orange.

All the cases regardless of their composition were manufactured in standard sizes to accommodate the average sizes of the daguerreotype, ambrotype or tintype. There was a slight variation among manufacturers in the outside dimensions.

Case manufacturers were generally not identified except in the photos of Mathew Brady and John Plumbe Jr. Before the appearance of manufactured cases, photographers built their own.

Tip

Other than the construction of the cases, one of the best ways to date a case is through surface design. Initially case designs were based on Greek and Roman forms, such as the lyre. In the 1840s nature subjects were popular, such as fruits, birds, marine life and flowers. The rose motif had at least thirty variations from 1844 to 1850.

The intricate designs of the union case allowed artists to create designs

STANDARD CASE STYLES	
Style	**Average size**
Whole	7″ × 9″
Half	5″ × 6″
Quarter	4″ × 5″
Sixth	3½″ × 3¾″
Ninth	2½″ × 3″
Sixteenth	2″ × 2″

based on famous paintings. The increase in Catholic immigration to the United States popularized Christian religious scenes prior to the Civil War. During the Civil War nationalistic themes increased. Other scenes were influenced by photographic trends; the availability of post-mortem photography gave rise to themes related to death. Home scenes depicting domestic bliss such as couples playing chess or family scenes were also common.

The other part of a cased image that can help you draw conclusions about the date of the image is the mat. Just as case designs changed during the years of cased images so did mat design. Mats came in several different styles such as fire-gilt, engraved, stamped or common. Acids were applied to the surface so that the appearance was frosted or marked or a pebble or sand finish. The mats were then lacquered. In the 1840s the octagon shape was popular. In the 1850s mat designs become more elaborate. Popular styles were elliptical, nonpareil, double elliptical, ornate elliptical, oval, and ornate border.

FACTORS TO CONSIDER WHEN DATING A CASED IMAGE

Photographer's imprints: Daguerreotypists often followed the custom of painters by scratching their names into the metal plate.

Name on the brass mat, velvet interior of the case

Composition of case

Design on surface of case

Hinges

Mat shape and style

Tip

In order to date any features of the cases, it will be necessary to consult guidebooks. Three excellent ones to the history and design elements of the cases are Floyd and Marion Rinhart's *American Miniature Case Art* (New York: A.S. Barnes and Co., 1969); Paul Berg's *Nineteenth Century Photo-*

Printed Source

graphic Cases and Wall Frames (Huntington Beach, Calif.: Huntington Valley Press, 1995); and Clifford and Michele Krainik with Carl Walvoord's *Union Cases: A Collector's Guide to the Art of America's First Plastic* (Grantsburg, Wisc.: Centennial Photo Service, 1988). All the books are heavily illustrated with all known cases. The Rinharts include biographies of the case makers and engravers. They also created charts of the case sizes offered by various manufacturers. You can date a case by comparing it to the illustrations and charts used in these reference books. Each author has outlined when particular cases were popular and who manufactured them.

THREE

Paper Prints and Negatives

"Card portraits, as everyone knows, have become the social currency, the 'green-backs' of civilization."

—Oliver Wendell Holmes, 1863

I n the 1850s our ancestors could select the method of photography for their portrait. The daguerreotype, ambrotype, tintype and card photograph were available. Some of these processes were on the decline while others were just coming to the public's notice. Studios advertised the types of images they could produce. Photographers needed to be equally proficient in all the techniques in order to survive.

By the end of the 1860s, card photographs became the preeminent medium for portraits and the dominance of the paper print was established. Paper prints developed at the same time as the daguerreotype, but did not achieve popularity until the process of making multiple prints was introduced. Like many of the early processes, the paper print was invented in Europe and later came to the United States.

Daguerreotypes and ambrotypes began to disappear in favor of the print. Inexpensive to produce, durable and available in quantity, the paper image remains the primary photographic process even today.

TALBOTYPES: THE FIRST PAPER PRINT

The first paper print was the Talbotype. While Daguerre was developing the daguerreotype, an Englishman named Talbot was busy developing a process for fixing an image on paper. Named after their creator, Fox Talbot, these images never enjoyed the popularity of the daguerreotype.

Talbotypes, also known as calotypes, are very rare. Talbot ensured his own failure when he required strict patent enforcement.

Definitions

Talbotypes can be easily identified. The print was produced from a waxed paper negative. The images lack sharpness and clarity due to the poor quality of paper used for both the print and the negative.

CARD PHOTOGRAPHS

Definitions

The most popular type of paper print was the card photograph. It is essentially a paper print mounted on cardboard stock. Cartes de visite, cabinet cards and stereographs are three types of card photograph. The size of the card varied from cartes de visite which were 2½″ × 4″ to the Imperial or life-size cabinet cards which were 6⅞″ × 9⅞″. There were at least twenty different types of cards. The majority of cards in your collection are probably cartes de visite or cabinet cards. By the 1880s cabinet cards replaced the smaller cards in popularity.

Cartes de visite derive their name from the request of a member of a royal family who went to his photographer and asked for photographs the size of calling cards. They began appearing in the United States in 1860.

Important

In family photograph collections there may be an album of nineteenth-century card photographs that may not be members of your family. Collecting cards of royalty and other famous individuals became a pastime encouraged by the mass production of photographs of newsworthy events and famous people. Booksellers, publishers and photographers sold them to augment their income. They could sell thousands of a popular image.

Definitions

Cartes de visite were primarily albumen prints. These prints consist of paper stock of various thicknesses coated with egg white. A photograph was taken by exposing a glass negative coated with collodion to light while in the camera. The negative would then be placed against the coated paper and left in sunlight. The exposure to the sun developed the picture. Washing the print in chemical baths and toning it with gold choloride gave albumen prints a brownish color. Unfortunately, these early prints tended to fade.

This photograph is actually a copy of a cased image taken at an earlier date.
Collection of the author

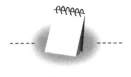

FAMILY PHOTO ALBUMS

Photograph albums initially appeared so that persons could collect autographs or visiting cards of friends or famous individuals. The carte de visite photograph created a new use for the albums: Instead of signatures, individuals could acquire photographs of visitors, friends and celebrated persons.

Card photographs encouraged people to create albums as a memorial or as a form of entertainment. Individuals, usually women, inserted pictures in the cutouts provided in the albums. Albums resembled family bibles in size and formality with velvet or leather covers and gilt edging, but the rigid format of the albums did not allow for creativity.

Tintype albums offered the first departure from the traditional. The thumbnail or gem-sized pictures required a new type of album. Similar in design to the other books, gem albums fit in the palm of the hand with different styles of cutouts.

In the 1880s with the introduction of candid photography, albums with plain paper pages became available. No longer was the creator confined by the layout dictated by the design. Suddenly albums fashioned by amateur photographers presented a personal view of the world in which they lived. The arrangement and placement of images tell us about the temperament and personality of the maker.

Albums were cooperative creations. The subject(s) posed for the camera, the photographer took the images, and the collector placed them in the album. The photographer and the collector may not have been the same person. Young women spent leisure time creatively laying out photographs in an expressive manner.

Candid photographs required a different type of album. Albums with pages of heavy black or white paper sewn together replaced the earlier types of albums. Individuals could lay out their images in any arrangement and add captions or scrapbook materials such as clippings. Photographs could be cut into any shape and placed creatively in the album.

Victorian photograph albums offer insights into the world in which our ancestors lived. Individuals no longer needed to visit a studio to have a picture taken. The technology allowed amateur photographers to record their daily lives. Individuals were no longer just photographed in their Sunday best, but were depicted in the process of work and play.

When examining the albums in your collection, pay attention to the individuals who are included, but use your genealogical research to notice which people are missing. Gaps in the photographic record might coincide with a tragedy or change in the family situation. You might discover that one album only depicts the college years of an ancestor, while another is an ongoing record of a life. Both men and women spent time creating albums or scrapbooks of their

---

FAMILY PHOTO ALBUMS (Continued)

lives, although more women entertained themselves with these projects. John Hutchins Cady, a Brown University student, created a series of albums during his college years. He made his albums out of cloth and embroidered the edges with needlework before adding the images. His albums are a wonderful view of the life of a student in the 1880s.

CARD PHOTOGRAPHS AND SIZES		
Boudoir	5¼″ × 8½″	Not known
Cabinet Card	4½″ × 6½″	1866
Carte de visite	4¼″ × 2½″	Process introduced in U.S. 1859
Imperial (life-size)	6⅞″ × 9⅞″	Not known
Panel	8¼″ × 4″	Not known
Promenade	4″ × 7″	1875
Stereograph	Either 3″ × 7″ or 4″ × 7″	Smaller 1859; larger 1870
Victoria	3¼″ × 5″	1870

It is possible to establish an approximate date for a card photograph based on the distinct size of the card. A more exact date can only be determined based on other information contained in the image.

Unfortunately, identifying the photographic process used for a card photograph can be difficult unless you are trained in the methods of photo identification under a microscope. The nineteenth-century paper prints are a rainbow of colors from the brilliant blue of cyanotypes to the soothing gray of platinum prints. The color may also depend on the toning that has been used to tint the image. There are so many different types of prints that telling them apart is difficult.

Important

Stereographs

A stereoscopic image is two nearly identical images mounted side by side. A special camera with two lenses mounted two and one-half inches apart took the picture. The distance between the lenses matches the average distance between two eyes. This calculation allows the image to become three-dimensional when examined through a special viewer.

\di'fin\ *vb*

Definitions

Stereoscopic images could be created in any photographic medium, but they are primarily paper prints mounted on a cardboard stock.

The purpose of the stereograph was to provide entertainment. A few companies produced sets of images on different subjects. These included travel, wartime scenes, transportation and religious subjects.

DATING THE CARD STOCK OF STEREOGRAPHS Square corners	
Color	**Date**
White, cream or gray lustrous	1854-1862
Dull gray	1860-1863
Canary yellow, chrome yellow	1862-1868
Blue, green, red, violet	1865-1870
Rounded corners	
Type	**Date**
Photographs; colors in chart for square corners, above	1868-1882
Copied photographs	1873-1878
Printed	1874-1878
Card mounts, curved, actual photographs	
Color	**Date**
Buff mounts, thick card	1879-1906
Gray mounts	1893-1940
Black mounts	1902-1908

For More Info

Data in these charts are based on information presented in William C. Darrah's *Stereoviews: A History of Stereographs in America and Their Collection* (Gettysburg, Pa.: Times and News Publishing, 1964).

Our ancestors collected stereographs for entertainment. *Collection of the author*

TYPE OF STEREOGRAPHS	
Daguerreotypes	1850–1854
Glass	1854–1862
Porcelain	1854–1858
Card	1854–1938

The reverse side of the card usually contained a label with information on the photographer or publisher, the title and subject. This is very helpful when trying to date the image.

CANDID PHOTOGRAPHY

Candid photography was introduced by Kodak in the 1880s. *Collection of the author*

In the 1880s a new type of paper print appeared. While studios produced all card photographs, individuals created the new pictures. The age of amateur photography began with the slogan, "You push the button, we do the rest." George Eastman developed an easy to use roll-film camera that could be used by anyone. He called it the Kodak.

Amateur photographers could take as many as one hundred pictures per roll with the first models. After taking an image, the photographer turned a key to move the film to a new exposure. Individuals no longer had to use chemicals and film. Each camera contained a roll of film. When all the pictures were taken, the photographer sent the camera back to the factory for processing. Later improvements allowed the photographers to load the film themselves and send it for development without the camera.

It was the wide availability of these cameras that helped create the majority of photographs in our family collections. The cameras were easy to use and inexpensive. Our ancestors found themselves free to pose and clown in front of the camera, recording memorable events and playful activities.

The size of the images varied according to the type of box camera used. The film and the cameras remained in use in families for generations. For instance Kodak roll-film 101 introduced in 1895 with a picture area of $3\frac{1}{2}'' \times 3\frac{1}{2}''$ wasn't discontinued until 1956. **While you might be able to establish the date of earliest use for a particular sized photograph, it is the information in the image that will ultimately provide a date.**

Handling Suggestions: *Don't Write on the Image*

Important credos when working with photographs are don't do anything that cannot be undone and don't write on the image. The best intentions to record information can inflict damage.

In the process of writing on the back of an image, many a family historian has left a lasting impression on the picture. The ink or pencil has bled through from the reverse to the front. The pressure points of writing become apparent. Even if the ink does not affect the image immediately, it will eventually leave a mark.

It is also possible while writing on the back of a print to inadvertently crack or otherwise damage the mount and the image. The paper backing on the image becomes fragile over time and breaks under the slightest pressure.

A good way to record information about a photograph is to place it in a transparent archival sleeve and label the sleeve not the image. Basic identifying information should include name and date. Labels for scenic photographs should also include the place.

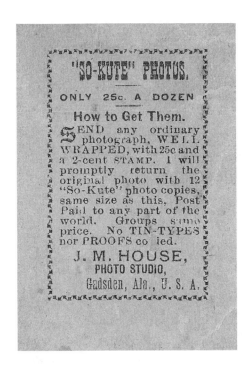

Use care when dating photographs. Photographers often copied older images using the latest technique. *Collection of the author*

NEGATIVES

Prior to collodion negatives in the 1860s, the number of lenses on a camera limited the quantity of prints that could be produced. With the discovery of the negative process there was no longer any limit. Since all prints in the nineteenth century were actually contact prints, the dimension of the negative determined the size of the picture. A contact print is produced when a negative is placed on a light-sensitive surface.

Negatives consist of a support surface and a coating of a light-sensitive material such as collodion, gelatin, nitrocellulose or cellulose acetate. The support for the negative surface can be glass or film.

The vast majority of nineteenth-century negatives were glass. Glass negatives were either wet plate or dry plate. Wet-plate negatives had to be damp when used. Photographers made them immediately prior to use by coating glass with collodion. The dry-plate process revolutionized photography. Photographers could buy their materials ready-made instead of preparing the surfaces themselves. The amount of equipment necessary to take photographs was substantially reduced.

\di'fin\ *vb*

Definitions

CHARACTERISTICS OF GLASS NEGATIVES		
Collodion, also known as Wet Plate	Thick glass; edges ground; gray coating; produced by individual photographer	1851-c. 1880
Gelatin dry plate	Thin glass; uniform thickness; edges sharp; black coating; factory produced	c. 1880-c. 1920

The film negatives that we use today began with the Kodak process of the 1880s. The support surface was a type of clear plastic and the negative material varied.

Home photograph collections may or may not contain negatives. If you have film negatives in your family materials, examine them carefully.

CHARACTERISTICS OF FILM NEGATIVES		
Eastman American Film-gelatin	Brittle; edges uneven	1884-c. 1890
Roll Film-clear plastic	Nitrocellulose; thin; curls and wrinkles easily	1889-1903
Roll Film-clear plastic	Coated on both sides with gelatin to prevent curling	1903-1939
Sheet Film-clear plastic	Machine-cut sheet; rectangular; edges stamped Eastman	1913-1939
Roll Film-clear plastic	Cellulose acetate; marked safety on the edge	1939-present

Help for Identifying Negatives

Identifying the type of negative in your collection and the time period in which it was used is easier than identifying nineteenth-century prints. This chart is a guide to negatives based on their characteristics. Bear in mind that photographers often used up supplies they had on hand before moving on to a new medium. The end dates of usage may not be firm.

Handling Suggestions: *Fragile and Dangerous*

Warning

When dealing with film negatives, it is important to examine them carefully because they may be chemically unstable. A nitrocellulose, or nitrate, negative that was popular between 1889 and 1939 is a safety hazard. Museums and archives copy and destroy these negatives due to a danger of spontaneous combustion. The risk to the home family collection may not be as great unless there is a large quantity of these negatives in your home stored in an area with temperature fluctuations like an attic.

You can identify nitrate negatives by doing the following:
- Examine the edge of the negative to see if the word *safety* appears. If it doesn't, the negative may be nitrate.
- Using a pair of scissors, snip off a small section of the negative and place in a nonflammable container such as an ashtray.
- Try to ignite the section using a match. If it burns, it is nitrate; if it doesn't, it is unmarked safety film.
- A reputable photo conservation lab can copy nitrate film. This film cannot be sent through the mail because it is considered a fire hazard.
- Ask your local fire department how to dispose of the negatives.

DATING PAPER PRINTS

Paper prints can be dated by identifying the photographic process and by noting the thickness of the paper on which it is mounted. One expert on card photographs suggests that dating card stock, using identifiers such as color, shape of corners and type of image, is highly accurate plus or minus a couple of years.

CHARACTERISTICS OF DIFFERENT PRINTS		
Type of Photograph	**Date Introduced**	**Characteristics**
Albumen Print	1855	Fades; tiny cracks in the image; colors same as salted paper print; paper fibers visible
Carbon Print	1860	No fading; large cracks in dark areas
Cyanotype	1880	Blue
Gelatin Developing Out	1885	No paper fibers; reflective dark areas resemble a silver color
Gelatin Printing Out Paper or Collodion	1885	Purple image; no paper fibers visible
Matte Collodion	1894	No fading; some paper fibers visible
Platinotype	1880	No fading
Salted Paper Print	1840	Yellow-brown, red-brown; fades
Woodburytype	1866	No fading; some cracking in dark areas

TAX STAMPS

Another helpful clue for dating card photographs is the presence of a stamp on the back of the image. On 1 August 1864, the United States government levied a tax on photographs. A revenue stamp was applied to the reverse of the photograph. Photographers were required to hand cancel each stamp with name or initials and date of sale. The law was repealed 1 August 1866. Handwritten dates reflect the exact day the photograph was sold. For more on this topic, see Kathleen Fuller's "Civil War Stamp Duty: Photography as a Revenue Source," in *History of Photography* 4 (October 1980): 263–282.

Dating paper prints can be difficult due to the wide variation in size and process. The best way to establish a time frame for an image is through the clues present in the image.

Revenue stamps can help you date a photograph.
Collection of the author

Notes

TAX STAMP RATES

2¢ on photographs selling for less than 25¢

3¢ on photographs selling for 25¢ to 50¢

5¢ on photographs selling for 50¢ to $1

5¢ on photographs selling for each additional $1

FOUR

Color Photographs

"The fact is, none of us sufficiently appreciate[s] the nobleness and sacredness of colour."

—Alfred A. Wall, *A Manual of Artistic Colouring, as Applied to Photographs: A Practical Guide to Artists and Photographers* (London: Thomas Piper, 1861):i

As you look at your family photographs, you will see a variety of colored images. Some will be hand-colored. In some cases the image will have just the details such as jewelry or collars enhanced, while in others the original photograph is underneath overpainting. One popular form of nineteenth-century portraits appears at first glance to be a charcoal drawing; however, upon close inspection, you can see that the charcoal is actually just outlining the photograph.

The information contained in the hand-colored image or color print can help you date and interpret your collection. The coloring itself cannot date a hand-colored image, but it can show you the color of someone's eyes. **A color print, however, can be dated by the technique by which it was produced.**

Tip

Although we take color for granted as a medium for family photographs, it was virtually unavailable a generation ago. Until Kodak introduced amateur color photography in 1936, photographers had to use a variety of techniques to add color to images. Many studios employed colorists to highlight details or enhance images.

HAND-COLORING

As early as 1841 photographers were seeking methods to add color to their images. As much as the popular press discussed the virtues of the daguerreotype they criticized the absence of color. Photographers sought ways to increase the realism of their images. Since the production of a color image was not yet possible, they improvised. Artistic mediums such as colored powders, watercolors, oil paints, crayons and charcoal were used.

Photographer's imprints alluded to hand-coloring services. *Collection of the author*

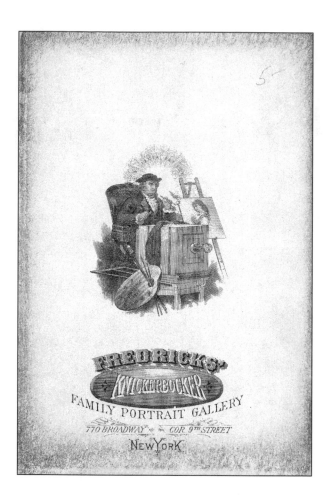

Hand-coloring accomplished several things. Early photographers wanted to impress their customers with high-quality images and color was a way to satisfy them. Adding color created contrast and improved upon any imperfections present in the image. Since early paper prints had a tendency to fade, colorists used charcoal to trace the image. Overpainting with a variety of substances could also be utilized to reduce fading.

Colorists, usually artists, would add color to photographs to emphasize certain details. In some cases, so much color was added it is difficult to determine whether the pictures are paintings or photographs. In reality, they are hybrids, combining elements of both media. You may have images in your collection that appear to be paintings but are actually hand-colored images.

There were many different methods used to color photographs. Manuals contained specific instructions on what features to color. For instance, the face could be improved by emphasizing the cheeks, nostrils, the bridge of the nose, brow and chin. Other commonly colored parts of a photograph were the hands, draperies, clothing and background of the image.

The palette of colors depended on what was being colored. For example, jewelry and buttons were enhanced with gold, while pink was added to cheeks. Skilled technicians would add color to clothing. Everything from white collars to plaid garments could be improved with a little color. In one family's collection a black-and-white photograph contains the photographer's hand-coloring instructions: "dark grey eyes, light golden hair, golden brown velvet suit, pearl buttons, cream collar and cuffs, and green peach leaves in hand."

Different photographic methods required different types of coloring techniques. A daguerreotype's metal surface could be enhanced with colored powders. They could be applied by using a brush or by gently blowing the colors onto the surface. Paper prints were easier to color than daguerreotypes since it was a traditional painting surface. The tools used were the same as those for painting portraits: brushes and colors. In a few examples, photographic artists added individuals to the original photograph.

In this portrait the shirt is colored white to contrast in the image.
Collection of the author

RETOUCHING

The need for enhancements increased with the introduction of larger prints. A slight flaw that was barely visible in a carte-de-visite portrait was a major imperfection in the larger card photographs.

Photographers used retouching to eliminate bothersome flaws in negatives. It was more economical to fix the negative before prints were made. Pinpoint flaws in the negative could be filled in with pencil or charcoal. Retouching could eliminate minor blemishes, stray hairs and distractions, while major changes to the negative could be induced by actually scraping away some of the emulsion. In this way, significant changes to the original image could be introduced without damaging the photograph.

COLOR PHOTOGRAPHY

While processes such as chromolithography introduced color into printing, it wasn't until the twentieth century that color photography became available. The first color printed images appeared in the mid-nineteenth century. The beginnings of color negatives and prints have their roots in the printing industry.

In 1862, a Frenchman, Louis Ducos du Hauron, proposed that red, yellow and blue are basic colors and that all other colors are combinations of them. He designed a camera that used mirrors to produce three separate negatives in different colors. The first color lithographs were made from his three-color process of red, green and violet. Chromolithographs appeared as advertising and in magazine work.

It wasn't until 1904 that the first commercially successful color process was introduced. Developed by Auguste and Louis Lumière, it was called the Autochrome. This process used starch grains dyed red, green and blue to create a positive image. The process was easy to use. A photographer could insert the plate in the camera, expose it to light and develop it. A special viewer called a diascope could be used to view the transparency. Photographs of scenes and individuals could be taken, but unfortunately this

\di'fin\ *vb*

Definitions

For More Info

FOR FURTHER DISCUSSION

For more on color photography see *A Half Century of Color*, by Louis Walton Sipley (New York: Macmillan Co., 1951) and *Kodachrome and How to Use It*, by Ivan Dmitri (New York: Simon & Schuster, 1940).

For More Info

FOR FURTHER DISCUSSION

For a more complete discussion of the stability of color photographs, see *The Permanence and Care of Color Photographs: Traditional and Digital Color Prints, Color Negatives, Slides, and Motion Pictures*, by Henry Wilhelm (Grinnell, Iowa: Preservation Publishing Company, 1993).

Warning

process was used by professional photographers and rarely appears in family collections.

For another three decades, color photography remained a commercial venture in the hands of professional photographers and printers. It wasn't until 1935 that the first amateur color film became available. It was Kodak's Kodachrome 16mm motion picture film. Reasonably priced for the home photographer, the retail price of a roll of film when first introduced was $7.75 for 100 ft. In 1936 Kodachrome became available in an 8mm format and as slides.

Negative film became available from Kodak in 1941. This was the first color still film not intended for the commercial market. Just as the early daguerreotypists advised individuals to wear certain colors to obtain a good likeness, so did Kodak. The company printed a manual to guide family photographers. It contained a chart of acceptable clothing colors and background choices. The reason for this instruction was that the intensity of Kodacolor could be distracting if bright colors were worn against a colorful background.

Polaroid

In 1947 Edwin Land patented a process for producing black-and-white pictures that developed in a minute. This meant amateur photographers did not have to send their film to a lab for developing. The quality of what was captured on film could be judged immediately and re-shot if necessary. Initially offered as a black-and-white process, it wasn't until the 1970s that Polaroid's color film was available to the public. Close to 65 percent of the billion Polaroid pictures taken in 1974 would be color. Most of them were family photographs. Polaroid maintained its appeal to amateur photographers by offering new, improved cameras every few years.

By examining the color images in your collection, you may be able to date an image by its type. In the case of Polaroid pictures, different films were used in various camera models. You can date an instant image by its size, shape and type.

Handling Suggestions

There are a few guidelines to follow with your color family photographs so that they can be around for future generations. Color photography is an unstable medium, and it needs to be properly stored in order to extend its lifetime. The life span of a typical color image is estimated at twenty-five years. A Polaroid will last for only five to ten years.

1. **Do not expose images to sunlight.** If you want to display a photograph, make a copy from the original negative or photograph and use that. Sunlight accelerates deterioration by attacking the dyes in the color film.
2. Store them in a dark place with a stable environment. The best place to store color materials is in a cold place at a stable temperature in the range of 30° F. Two storage considerations are low temperature and

humidity. Since this type of environment is not available for most home collections, it is important to keep images in an area without fluctuating temperature and humidity.

3. **Retain the negatives.** Since prints will become discolored over time, it is important to retain the negatives so that new prints can be made.

Important

FIVE

Looking for Clues

"To consider photography a mere mechanical art is a great mistake . . . photography to be successful requires expensive apparatus . . ."

—Coleman and Remington, Photographic Artists, 25 Westminster St., Providence. From the Rhode Island Historical Society

Important

Tip

While the type of photograph may place the image in a time period, the internal clues will narrow down the date. **By carefully examining all the details present in the picture and recording them on a worksheet, you can develop the story of the photograph.** In a portrait, facial characteristics can help you identify an image while the choice of props and backgrounds provide insight into the personality of the sitter.

Photographs of interior or exterior scenes contain many items that help you date the image. For instance, to date an interior scene you can research the decorative details. **It is the presence or absence of certain elements that can date street scenes.** The technological details of an exterior scene are particularly helpful such as light fixtures, trolley lines and paved streets. If a street scene has electric lights, then you can research when lighting was installed in that part of town. Dating the style of architecture can also place the image in a time frame. The easiest detail to research in a street scene is signage. For some searches you will have to enlist the help of other individuals in your quest for information on the image. It may be necessary to correspond with relatives or to contact experts to help you establish a date.

FAMILY RESEMBLANCES

Probably the most difficult technique of photo identification involves facial characteristics. In some families, for instance, there may be a distinguishing characteristic such as a mole that appears in a particular part of the face in several family members or the shape of the eyes or nose. Hopefully your collection of photographs contains some identified images, so that you can begin to group them by family facial characteristics.

Tip

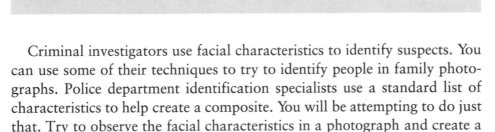

DETAILS TO LOOK FOR IN AN IMAGE

Facial characteristics

Props

Architecture

Technological details (streetlights, trolleys, etc.)

Signage

Criminal investigators use facial characteristics to identify suspects. You can use some of their techniques to try to identify people in family photographs. Police department identification specialists use a standard list of characteristics to help create a composite. You will be attempting to do just that. Try to observe the facial characteristics in a photograph and create a table of things to look for.

If you trace a photocopy of a family portrait and reduce it to the scale of the photo you are trying to identify, you can compare jaws, ears and facial shape. **Be careful with this method of identification, however, because a person's face changes with age and weight increases or decreases.**

Using the identified images in your collection, lay them out in a photo timeline by person. Then compare your unidentified images to the timelines. This will establish a family connection. Those images that defy identification will require further research.

When you create your photographic timeline, it may help to use

Important

PHYSICAL CHARACTERISTICS TO LOOK AT

In particular it is helpful to look at:

Shape of face (oval, heart-shaped, round, square)

Eyes (shape, position, color, size)

Nose and nostrils (shape, position, size)

Ears (shape, size, position on head, length)

Hair pattern (baldness, widow's peak)

Eyebrows (size, shape)

Moles

Teeth

Tip

Use care when comparing facial characteristics; a person's face changes over time.
Lynn Betlock

photocopies of the images. In this way you can retain the original layout of the collection as it was arranged by the owner. Reexamining the photographs in the context in which they were given to you by the original owner can help you identify individuals.

Relatives can be very helpful with facial identification. If members of the person's generation are still living, you might want to enlist their help. They may recognize the individual in the photograph. Even if the name eludes them, they may be able to offer additional clues. The props and backgrounds apparent in the image may help your relatives identify the person in the photograph.

PROPS AND BACKDROPS

Props could include photographs of family members not present. *Collection of the author*

Studio photographers placed their customers in a setting through the use of props and backdrops. Photographers kept a supply of props on hand, such as toys, books, flowers, drapery and columns. Their purpose was to add interest to the picture. People could also supply their own props. In some cases they add significance. For instance, a woman posed in mourning clothes with a man's photograph may be including her deceased husband in the portrait. Occupational portraits contain some clue regarding the subject's employment.

The appearance of the first painted backdrop in a photograph in the 1840s coincides with the popularity of the daguerreotype. Backdrops provided the context for the props. Studios employed artists to create backdrops similar to the ones used in the theater. With the appropriate props, a visit to the photographer could transport the customers into another world.

Many photo studios used theatrical backdrops and props in their photographs.
New England Historic Genealogical Society

Frontier scenes, landscapes and architecture can be seen in nineteenth-century images. The backdrop could substitute for actual props and show individuals appearing to pose with items that are actually only painted surfaces, such as architectural details like balustrades. Creative photographers would set props against an appropriate background painting. People could pose with bicycles in front of a landscape or appear to be riding in a car in an outdoor setting.

Props and backdrops are not just useful for dating an image. **The choice of backgrounds and items can provide clues into the character and personality of your ancestors.** They could manipulate the setting of a photograph to create a sense of fantasy or comedy. People could have their photograph taken while miming an activity using materials they brought with them or that the photographer had on hand. Young men in the late nineteenth century liked to be portrayed as fun-loving. Portraits often show them clowning for the camera.

Tip

INTERNAL INFORMATION

Dating and identifying exterior scenes is not a subjective process; you will be able to date many of the visible details through library research. **Use a**

Tip

magnifying glass to examine the image for particular items that can be dated, such as business signs, architecture and technological elements. Each one of these elements can be researched further.

Signage can be verified by consulting city directories. This will tell you when a company was in business and where it was located.

Architectural details can be researched by consulting photographs, books and maps. You can compare your image to other street scenes of the same location. By consulting a reference book on architecture you can establish when a particular style was popular. Maps illustrate when a neighborhood was developed.

Technological elements can be the final clue to dating an image. For instance, the condition of a street may be a clue. Many local histories mention when paving was introduced. They also provide dates for the installation of gas and electric lights. The presence of telegraph lines, railroad tracks, fire hydrants and bridges can also be dated.

Interior scenes should be carefully examined as well. The artifacts in the picture may be family heirlooms or a new purchase. Family-owned luxury items such as cameras, typewriters, binoculars, cars and bicycles are clues to both time period and owner.

If you are unable to date an artifact by consulting reference books, an antique dealer can provide direction. They are usually aware of collectors who can help. A curator at a local historical society or museum may be another good resource.

The following should be consulted when trying to date an artifact:
- Reference books
- Antique dealers
- Collectors
- Local historical societies or museums
- Family members

Sources

CASE STUDY: INTERNAL DETAILS

Case Study

In the street scene of Providence, Rhode Island, on page 43, two elderly gentlemen rest on the doorstep of a building. A brief penciled caption on the reverse of the image reads "Charles St." There are a few business signs in the image that may help date it.

The internal details help narrow down the time period of the photograph. The presence of trolley tracks, telephone lines and cobblestone streets suggest that the photograph was taken after 1894. A history of the city of Providence verifies that telephone service was introduced in the city in 1881. The streets were laid with cobblestones between 1864 and 1880. Another clue to the time period is the installation of electric trolley tracks from 1892 to 1894. In 1910 this particular type of trolley support pole was replaced.

A good next step is to research the four signs that appear in the photograph. The most easily read sign is for the Boston Dye House. City directory research for 1894-1910 does not reveal any dye houses of that name. The

A date for a photograph can be established through the internal information present in the image. *Rhode Island Historical Society*

only other two businesses present in the image are a barbershop and a cigar store, but both are without names. There are several possibilities listed in the *Business Directory* for Providence, Rhode Island.

The last sign is in Yiddish. It took consultation with several individuals before the sign was deciphered. The sign refers to a business that sells books and religious articles.

A final date for the photograph is derived from information in a house directory, which is arranged by street address and lists who lived or worked at any given address. This showed that for the period 1894-1910 there was only one dyer, an Israel Levy, living on the right street. He was in business from 1895 to 1897. The only year both a cigar shop and a barbershop operated in close vicinity was 1896.

See Also

Chapter 6, starting on page 44, has more information about city, regional and business directories.

SIX

Identifying the Photographer

"I got a fine likeness of my sister at Whipple's last week . . ."

—Letter from Caroline Cushman to Henry Wyles Cushman. From the Cushman Collection in the New England Historic Genealogical Society

I dentifying a photographer's dates and places of operation is the most straightforward task involved in photo research. These two little pieces of information can help you place an ancestral portrait within a particular time period. When this data is pieced together with your research on other clues in the image, it may enable you to name the individual in the picture.

PHOTOGRAPHER'S IMPRINT

A photographer's imprint will allow you to trace the business dates for that individual or studio. There are many different varieties of imprints including handwritten, embossed labels, and rubber-stamped identifications. Photographers could order preprinted cards from their paper supplier or place the imprint on the card themselves.

Many of the images in your family collection will have a photographer's imprint on the stock to which the image is mounted. It is important to know where to look for an imprint.

Cased images can have the photographer's name scratched into the plate or glass. Photographers also used symbols or business cards to identify their work. Their name may also appear on the brass mat or embossed into the velvet interior in the case.

With paper mounts, the photographer's imprint may appear stamped or embossed on the mat or be handwritten. Card photographs can have imprints on either the front or back of the card. If a card photograph lacks an imprint, it may be a copy of an original card.

Important

44

TYPES OF IMPRINTS

1. Embossed or impressed

2. Paper labels or stamps

3. Handwritten

4. Rubber-stamped name, address and sometimes the logo of the photographer

5. Printed name and address

The imprint does not always refer to a photographer. It can be the name of a publisher or distributor. Many businesses sold card photographs published by companies other than the original photographer. The most popular were portraits of important individuals such as royalty and newsworthy events such as the Civil War.

It is more difficult to locate the imprint on prints or negatives. Occasionally, a photographer may have scratched his name into the emulsion on the negative, but this is the exception. Paper prints, other than card photographs, can contain an embossed imprint, but identification is usually stylistic rather than preprinted.

Generally an imprint identifies the name of the studio, publisher or pho-

Tip

WHERE TO FIND IMPRINTS

Cased Images (Daguerreotypes, Ambrotypes, Tintypes):

Name may be scratched into a plate or the emulsion similar to an artist's identification on a painting.

Name on the brass mat or velvet interior side of the case.

Paper Mounts:

Handwritten, embossed, or stamped on the mat.

Card Photograph:

On the front or back of the card.

Paper Prints:

Not usually signed.

Negatives:

Scratched into the emulsion.

Imprints provide data that can assist in establishing when a photographer was in business. *Collection of author*

Definitions

"Mug books" is a slang term for a county history or biographical encyclopedia where people paid a fee to have their family or themselves included.

tographer. The simplest ones tell just the name of the photographer, usually an initial and a surname. The more elaborate can contain a list of services offered, awards received and photographer's logo. In cases where only a surname appears, you will have difficulty researching that photographer. The same is true for imprints that only list the company name without the proprietor's name. An address will enable you to place a photographer geographically and chronologically. A specific house or building and street number can narrow the search. An award or patent number will specify a date. Each additional piece of information is another detail to be researched.

Often an imprint will mention a partnership or the prior owner of the studio. This will assist you in trying to locate the dates of operation. Partnerships were usually short-lived and photographers, unless they had a steady clientele and solid reputation, moved around looking for better economic opportunities.

Sometimes imprints contain misspellings or a change in the spelling of the photographer's name. This can lead to difficulties in finding documentation. If you don't find what you are looking for the first time, try again searching for similar names.

RESEARCHING A PHOTOGRAPHER

Once you have a name, there are several basic resources for locating photographers. City directories, business directories, newspapers, almanacs, mug books or booster books (biographical encyclopedias of important members of a community), photography magazines and census records can all be utilized to locate photographers. Unfortunately, none of these sources are complete, so consult a few before declaring an end to your search. According

Information in a photographer's imprint can help you date an image. *Collection of the author*

VARIETY OF INFORMATION IN AN IMPRINT

Name	Price schedules
Address	Instructions for the sitter
Partnerships	Date of establishment
Logos	Names of retouchers
Patent numbers or license to use a process	Additional occupations
	Fraternal or religious affiliations
Special services	National origins
Negatives on file	Awards
Business sold to another photographer	Advertising

to a study of Pennsylvania photographers, directories list approximately 90.5 percent of the photographers.

Directories appear in several formats: by locality, region, business or house. Directories of a particular city or town appeared annually in larger cities and every few years in smaller towns. Regional or suburban listings usually included several small towns in their coverage area. Business directories contained information on the companies in the area covered by the publication. These are excellent sources for locating photographers. A typical listing will contain a person's name and address, occupation and often the name of his employer. When researching photographers, this data con-

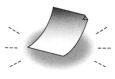

SOURCES TO FIND PHOTOGRAPHERS

Directories

Newspapers (news and obituaries)

Mug books

Court records

Census records, federal and state

Special census schedules

Photography magazines

Directories of regional photographers

Definitions

In some areas, a house directory may be called a householder's directory, reverse directory or criss-cross directory. It may be part of a city directory or a separate volume.

firms the information in the imprint. In some cases, it is possible to locate additional information by searching city directories page by page to locate the name of the business in addition to the name of the owner. Obviously, this method is time-consuming and should only be a last resort.

Another specialized publication is the house directory. It enables you to find the names of individuals or businesses with just an address. In cases where the imprint only includes the address and a business name, you can locate the name of the owner by using a house directory. Each listing is in order by the name of the street followed by the house or building number and the names of the occupants.

Your public library or local historical society probably has directories for your city or town. If you are researching someone outside the local area, it may require a little more effort to find the ones you are looking for. The two largest collections of city directories are in the Library of Congress and at the American Antiquarian Society in Worcester, Massachusetts.

You may be able to borrow the directories you need or hire a researcher in the vicinity of your research. The American Genealogical Lending Library (see listing on page 84) lends city directories on film or fiche to its members.

Another good source for finding photographers is directories of regional photographers in which you may find a full description of a photographer. This can save you a lot of time and effort.

Chris Steele and Ron Polito's exhaustively researched *A Directory of Massachusetts Photographers 1839-1900* (Camden, Me.: Picton Press, 1993) relied on city directories to track photographers through time. Each citation for a photographer is in three parts: business listings, residence address and advertisements. For instance, if you were researching a photograph taken by Oscar T. Higgins in Boston, you would notice that he operated out of several addresses from 1853 to 1865 and with different business partners:

1853	92 Hanover St.
1854	114 Hanover and 199 Hanover St.
1854	94 Hanover St.
1855–58	114 Hanover St.
1859	114 Hanover St.
1864–65	109 Washington St.

Included in the information that Steele and Polito discovered in the directory listings were the following partnerships: Welch & Higgins (1852–53); Higgins & Pushee (1859–1860); Higgins & Brothers (1860–61); Higgins & Whitaker (1861); Higgins & Collier (1862); Higgins & Company (1863–65); and Higgins, Chandler & Company (ca. 1860–70). If you were researching a photograph with the imprint Higgins & Whitaker, you would have a clue that the photograph was taken in 1861. Other information you collected on the image may support that conclusion.

Newspapers often carried photographers' advertisements, news items about them and their obituaries. **Unless the newspaper you are using is indexed, the material can be difficult to locate. This is a labor-intensive**

Timesaver

search and should be saved until you exhaust all other research options. Occasionally, a newspaper would run a story on a local studio, for instance, if someone famous visited to have a portrait taken or a new process was introduced.

Photographer Samuel Masury trained with one of America's first daguerreotypists, John Plumbe, whose skill with capturing images was well known. A reporter from a Providence, Rhode Island, newspaper heard that Masury opened a studio in the city and commented in an editorial on the images he took. "We have not seen any specimens of the art which we prefer to those of Mr. Masury." The date of this article establishes Masury as a photographer operating in Providence in January 1846.

The United States Newspaper Project is a special federally funded project to create a nationwide listing of newspapers published in each state. A central repository of newspapers in each state participating in the project can help you locate a newspaper for a particular area. In some localities, directories don't exist, but newspapers do. If you can find a newspaper for the town your photographer lived in, you may be able to obtain a microfilm reel through your local public library.

Printed Source

Subscription books, known as mug books or booster books, can be a tremendous help. They featured biographies of prominent individuals. If the photographer you are researching was well established in a locality, he may have contributed to a county or town history. These mug book sketches, often written by the person depicted, contain biographical information that can help you.

Publications created for a special purpose such as a centennial celebration are also good resources. They accepted advertising from local business and could feature a brief history of the studio in which you are interested.

Photography magazines of the period also published articles on studios and accepted advertising. By searching an index of these journals for all years a studio was operating, you may find additional information on the photographer. From an article in the *Photographic Art Journal*, Steele and Polito learned that Luther Holman Hale began his photography business on Milk Street in Boston. This information does not appear in any other source.

Federal and state census records can also assist you in the search for the dates a photographer was in business. The availability of census indexes on the Internet, in libraries, and through search services makes this information the most accessible. The population schedules of the census can be valuable tools for locating a photographer. By using census indexes to supply a volume and page number, you can then examine the photographer's census report.

Remember not to be misled when a photographer lists his occupation as something else, particularly in the early years of photography. Photographers often listed their occupation by the process in which they specialized. A variety of occupational titles included daguerreotypist, ambrotypist, tintypist, or even artist. An occupation was the way an individual defined

Reminder

Printed Source

NATIONAL PHOTOGRAPHIC PRESS

The Daguerreian Journal, 1850, continued by *Humphrey's Journal of Photography* until 1870

The Photographic Art Journal, 1851, bought out by *American Journal of Photography* (1852) in 1861

The Philadelphia Photographer, 1864-1888

The St. Louis Practical Photographer, 1877-1882

St. Louis Photographer (later the *St. Louis and Canadian Photographer*), 1883-1910

---

himself. A person with multiple occupations would have had to select one for the census taker.

Special censuses, or nonpopulation schedules, are helpful when available (see page 51). The Manufacturing or Industrial schedules from 1850 to 1870 include photographers. Their purpose was to compile information about manufacturing, mercantile, commercial and trading businesses that had a gross product income of more than five hundred dollars. The 1880 special schedule is known as the Manufacturing Schedule. Later schedules were destroyed. Information listed included name of business or owner; amount of capital invested; and quantity and value of materials, labor, machinery and products. Silas B. Brown, a Providence photographer, appeared in the 1860 census of industry. His product was ambrotypes; his occupation, photographic artist; his worth fifteen hundred dollars and he had five hundred picture frames, chemicals, cases and other materials in his possession. The census also states that he had two male employees that cost him seventy-five dollars per month in wages.

INTERNET SITES

While the majority of research on photographers is still accomplished using printed materials, there are also Internet resources to help with the process. Card catalogs for most major libraries are on-line, with the number increasing daily.

The George Eastman House, an international museum of photography, has made its database of photographers available on-line (http://www.eastman.org/4_educ/gehdata.html). Libraries and archives from all over the United States contributed information to this database. It chronicles everyone from the small-town photographer to the world-renowned. Search terms for the database include photographer, geographic location, subject and process. Specific information relating to business addresses is not avail-

TABLE OF 1850, 1860 AND 1870 SPECIAL CENSUS FOR INDUSTRY	
State	**Location of Originals**
Alabama	Alabama Department of Archives and History
California	California State Library, Sacramento, CA
Colorado (1870 only)	Duke University Library, Durham, NC
Connecticut	Connecticut State Library, Hartford, CT
Delaware	Delaware Public Archives Commission, Dover, DE
District of Columbia*	Duke University Library, Durham, NC
Florida*	Florida State University Library, Gainesville, FL
Idaho (1870 only)	Idaho Historical Society, Boise, ID
Illinois*	Illinois State Archives, Springfield, IL
Indiana	Indiana State Library, Indianapolis, IN
Iowa*	State Historical Society of Iowa Library, Des Moines, IA
Kansas* (1860, 1870)	Kansas State Historical Society, Topeka, KS
Kentucky*	Duke University Library, Durham, NC
Maine	Maine State Archives, Augusta, ME
Maryland* (1850,1860-Baltimore City, County only)	Department of Legislative Reference, City Hall, Baltimore, MD
Massachusetts*	Commonwealth of Massachusetts State Library and Archivist of the Commonwealth, Office of the Secretary of State (duplicates), Boston, MA
Michigan*	State Archives of Michigan, Lansing, MI
Minnesota	Minnesota Historical Society, St. Paul, MN
Mississippi	Mississippi Department of Archives and History, Jackson, MI
Missouri	State Historical Society of Missouri, Columbia, MO
Montana* (1870)	Montana Historical Society, Helena, MT
Nebraska* (1860,1870)	Nebraska State Historical Society, Lincoln, NE
New Hampshire	New Hampshire State Library, Concord, NH
New Jersey	New Jersey State Library, Trenton, NJ
New York	New York State Library, Albany, NY
North Carolina	North Carolina Department of Archives and History, Raleigh, NC
Ohio	State Library of Ohio, Columbus, OH
Oregon	Oregon State Library, Salem, OR
Pennsylvania*	NARA, Philadelphia, PA (Microfilm only)

TABLE OF 1850, 1860 AND 1870 SPECIAL CENSUS FOR INDUSTRY (Continued)	
State	**Location of Originals**
Rhode Island	Rhode Island State Archives, Providence, RI
South Carolina	South Carolina Archives Department, Columbia, SC
Tennessee*	Duke University Library, Durham, NC
Texas*	Texas State Library, Austin, TX
Vermont*	Vermont State Library, Burlington, VT
Virginia*	Virginia State Library, Richmond, VA
Washington* (1860, 1870)	Washington State Library, Olympia, WA
West Virginia* (1870)	West Virginia Department of Archives and History, Charleston, WV
Wisconsin	State Historical Society of Wisconsin, Madison, WI

* Microfilm available through the National Archives regional facilities in addition to those listed. See Lending Libraries, page 84, or page 103 for a list of regional National Archives facilities. (Chart taken from *Nonpopulation Census Schedules: Their Location,* compiled by Claire Pretchel-Kluskens, 1995.)

able through the database, but it will help you place a photographer in a location within a time frame.

City directories are also becoming available on-line through Primary Source Media (http://www.citydirectories.psmedia.com). The contents of this subscription database currently list directories for ninety-nine cities in the United States.

Internet Source

For individuals researching daguerreotypists, the premier resource for information on American photographers from 1839 to 1860 is Craig's Daguerreian Registry (http://www.daguerreotype.org). Craig has spent twenty-five years compiling this data. Collectors, dealers and other researchers have also submitted material for inclusion.

Researching photographers is challenging but can be rewarding. If you know the name of the photographer of that mysterious image in your collection, the material you locate on the photographer will supply you with one more clue.

CASE STUDY: TRACKING THE MANCHESTER BROTHERS

The search for the history of the Manchester Brothers, Providence, Rhode Island, is an example of what research can uncover about a photographer. The guidelines in the beginning of this chapter for identifying a photographer from an imprint and information in printed sources (see pages 44-50) will direct the research and help piece together background information on the two brothers.

Case Study

The first step is to examine actual images taken by them. The imprints embossed on the images show that the company was known by several names: Manchester and Chapin, Manchester Brothers, Manchester Brothers and Angell, and Manchester Bros. No other information appears in the imprint.

Two things are apparent from examining the images. First, they were taken by photographers from the daguerreotype era to at least the end of the nineteenth century. Second, at least some of the images are of notable Rhode Islanders.

A search of the city directories for Providence, Rhode Island, revealed the following information:

1850-1853	Edwin H. and H.N. Manchester, Daguerrean Artist, 33 Westminster St.
1853-1854	Manchesters and Chapin, 19 & 33 Westminster St.
1853-1859	Manchesters and Chapin, 73 Westminster St.
1860-1862	Manchester and Brother, 73 Westminster St.
1863	Manchester Brothers, 73 Westminster St.
1864	Manchester Brothers, 74 Westminster St.
1865	Manchester Brothers and Angell, 73 Westminster St.
1866-1868	Manchester Brother & Angell, 73 Westminster St.
1869-1878	Manchester Bros., 73 Westminster St.
1880	Manchester Bros., 329 Westminster St.

In addition to business addresses, the city directory listings provided the brothers' names, Edwin and Henry N., and their residential addresses. From the directories, the death of Henry N. is recorded as 24 November 1881. Directories are also useful to trace the development of a family. In this case, George E. Manchester joins the family business in 1878. By cross-checking the listing it is possible to obtain the names of the Manchesters' partners: Joshua Chapin, a doctor, and Daniel Angell.

From the information in the directories, the next step is to look for obituaries in the local newspaper, *The Providence Evening Bulletin*. The death indexes confirm the death date of Henry N., and provide one for his brother Edwin, 20 March 1904. The obituary of Edwin includes a photograph of him and establishes him as a brother to Henry with the middle initial H. The brothers operated a daguerreotype studio in approximately 1842 in Newport, Rhode Island. At an unspecified time, Edwin opened a studio in Pawtucket, Rhode Island, and Henry started one in Providence. The George E. listed in the directories is mentioned as his son.

Since Edwin's obituary states that the Manchesters were well known amongst the older families of Providence, the next step is to look at biographical encyclopedias. Henry Niles Manchester and Edwin Hartwell Manchester as well as one of their partners, Joshua Chapin, are mentioned in a mug book. This biographical information establishes that they were in Providence in 1844 working with another photographer, Samuel Masury, in both Providence and Woonsocket, Rhode Island. The brothers also continued to operate a studio in Newport during the summer season.

Since the encyclopedia mentions that they were one of the first studios to introduce the paper print to Rhode Island, **they might be mentioned in William S. Johnson's book, *Nineteenth Century Photography: An Annotated Bibliography, 1839-1879* (Boston: G.K. Hall & Co., 1990).** Johnson's book indexes images by photographers that appeared in nineteenth-century periodicals. One image is listed for the Manchester Brothers and one for the Manchester Brothers and Angell. Both woodcuts appeared in *Harper's Weekly* and depict famous Rhode Islanders.

Both Manchesters appear in census records, but that information did not challenge any of the material obtained from other sources. A search of newspaper indexes located a story about someone employed by the Manchesters. The article also included a narrative about meeting and photographing Edgar Allan Poe.

A duplication of this search using on-line databases illustrates the possibilities of this type of research. From Craig's Daguerreian Registry it is learned that Edwin was a daguerreian in Providence, Rhode Island from 1848 to 1860. A complete listing of business addresses and a partnership is part of his biography. The first new material for the Manchester Brothers is found in the citation for Henry Niles Manchester.

> First listed as a daguerreian in 1843 at 75 Court Street, Boston, Mass. This was the address of Plumbe's Gallery. In 1846 he was listed in Providence, R.I., at 13 Westminster Street, in business as Manchester, Thompson & Co. In 1847 he was listed alone at 33 Market Street. Another source has placed Manchester in business with Masury and Hartshorn in Boston.

The George Eastman House database did not yield any additional information. This database provides a span of dates of operation of photographer and location, but includes very few specifics. However, the *Index to American Photographic Collections: Compiled at the International Museum of Photography at George Eastman House*, by Andrew H. Eskind and Greg Drake (New York: G.K. Hall & Co., 3rd edition 1996), tells you where to find other collections of Manchester Brothers photographs.

By taking this research and applying it to the images with the Manchester Brothers' imprint, it is possible to approximate when a specific image was taken. For instance, a carte de visite with the imprint Manchester and Chapin would have been taken sometime between 1853 and 1859, while one with the imprint Manchester Brothers and Angell would have been taken between 1865 and 1868. Any further conclusions about the photographs will rely on the other methods of dating the image.

Printed Source

Notes

In the first citation, a woodcut of a portrait they took of Ida Lewis, Heroine of Newport, appeared in *Harper's Weekly* on 31 July, 1869. Ida Lewis became famous for single-handedly rescuing men drowning in the ocean outside the lighthouse in which she lived. The citation for Manchester Brothers and Angell also appeared as a woodcut in *Harper's Weekly* on 4 November, 1865. It was their portrait of Francis Wayland, a notable Rhode Island educator.

SEVEN

Images From Birth to Death

"Generally, a child will sit best if left entirely to the operator."

—Coleman and Remington, Photographic Artists, 25 Westminster St., Providence. From the Rhode Island Historical Society

Most family photograph collections document the stages of our ancestors' lives. Photographs in family collections usually fall into distinct categories: portraits, pictures of children, weddings, military service, school, vacations, holidays and other special events. Some collections contain images documenting the death of a family member. The elements of these family photographs such as composition and content can help you interpret the images in your collection. In some cases you will also be able to date the image based on these features. By looking at your family collection in terms of what was photographed, you can gain an understanding of what was important to your family.

PORTRAITS

The placement of sitters in the portrait can illuminate relationships within the family. Examine the portrait to determine who is the predominant individual. The dominant member of the family is usually the central figure. Traditionally, this is either the father or mother. The main figure can also be the individual who arranged for the portrait or the most successful member of the family. Young children and babies sit on the laps of the individuals in the front row. Who is standing in the back? Are the children arranged in birth order? Is there anyone absent from the photograph?

The style of a portrait can help you date the image. Each type of portrait was popular within a particular time frame. A type of portrait known as the vignette was the fashion from 1860 to 1870. The dating of portraits

Tip

Children were difficult to photograph. You can often see a mother holding a young child or infant. *David Lambert*

Reminder

depends on the size and the amount of the figure that is shown. This includes seated and standing figures.

Another element of portraits that can assign a date is the inclusion of a design in the picture. This can be an embossed frame around the image or just a plain window. Photographers sometimes placed the image within an ornamental background or cut it into a decorative shape. They had a wide variety of background patterns from which to choose. Some placed the portrait within a floral background while others appeared to be on a scroll.

Children

In the daguerreotype era it was difficult to take a good image of a child because of the long exposure time. Contraptions and techniques were developed to hold children still. It is sometimes possible to catch a glimpse of a person disguised under fabric or hidden behind a piece of equipment in the scene. Both techniques were employed to hold a child still. They were not always effective, however; blurry images of children and babies are quite common.

Weddings

Wedding photographs in the nineteenth century do not resemble the wedding photographs of today. **White wedding gowns were generally not worn because they were considered an unnecessary expense. Even if a bride wore**

A caption identifies this as "Aunt Ella's wedding dress."
Collection of the author

Most family collections contain wedding portraits. *Collection of the author*

a formal white gown, she would not be photographed in it, because early photographers did not always have the skill to photograph white or bright colors in any detail. Wedding portraits usually show the married couple in regular clothes or in their traveling garments.

The style of wedding portraits changed with the availability of images of royal weddings. These royal portraits could be purchased from booksellers and photographers. Victorian brides emulated the fashion and photographs of these royal couples for their own weddings. Victorian wedding albums usually included a group portrait of the participants, a static shot of the gifts and a portrait of the bride and groom.

Portraits of individuals in uniform provide clues to military service.
David Lambert

Military Service

The Civil War created a demand for images. Itinerant photography studios enabled soldiers to send their images home to their families. Soldiers also collected photos of members of their unit and sent them home with their letters. Unfortunately, many of the images of our Civil War ancestors are not good-quality images. In one unit a Sergeant Taylor wrote home, "I will

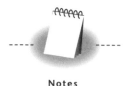

PHOTOGRAPHS AVAILABLE DURING THE CIVIL WAR 1861–1865

Daguerreotypes

Ambrotypes

Tintypes

Cartes de visite

Tip

Important

send you a thing that look a little like me, but not much. Don't be frightened nor let the children get scared at it."

The studio portraits that appear in many family collections are clues to military service. **By looking at uniforms, insignias and the photographer's identification in the portrait, one can begin to piece together additional information regarding rank or campaigns.**

Many family collections include battlefield scenes and portraits of officers. **Use care when identifying military images of the Civil War; the men depicted in the portraits may not be relatives.** Booksellers and photographers sold copies of significant events and people. For the soldiers and their families they could serve as a reminder of a particular battle.

In later wars, after the advent of amateur photography, soldiers or service personnel would create photograph albums of their activities and document their military service. One World War I nurse, Gertrude Bray, documented her travels and companions during the war in her photograph albums. Family collections usually contain at least some pictorial material relating to family military service.

School

There are many school photographs in family collections. Since the first class portrait was taken in 1840, schools have been taking photographs of their students and alumni. Some are group portraits of children posed in classrooms or in front of the school building, while others are individual portraits. It was popular in the late-nineteenth and early-twentieth century to pose for a formal graduation portrait. They are recognizable because young women dressed entirely in white. The most common prop was a rolled diploma.

Holidays

Families began photographing holiday celebrations when candid photography became available. In most family collections there are not only images of the family, but examples of cards sent to commemorate a holiday. These photographic cards provide the names of family members as well as close friends of the family. Those family friends may also have images of your family in their collection.

Our ancestors often posed for graduation portraits.
Collection of the author

Photographic greeting cards
are not new. *Collection of the
author*

Vacations

Our ancestors used photography to help them remember events in which
they participated. Your collection may contain images of picnics, family
outings and European vacations. Relatives would create albums out of images they had taken, or purchased, of their vacations.

Vacation photographs are
usually part of a collection.
Grant Emison

Postmortem

Postmortem or memorial photography was a common way of documenting the death of a member of the family. The tradition of photographing the deceased has a long history. Many wealthy families had after-death portraits painted of family members. When photography became available, it gradually replaced the painted postmortem portrait, although many daguerreotypes were taken for the purpose of commissioning a painting. With the advent of photography, it was possible for almost anyone to have an image of a deceased family member. Memorial photographs were commonly taken of children, and some of the images can be quite disturbing if you are not prepared to see a grieving mother holding her dead infant.

Some photographers specialized in postmortem photography. Children could be arranged on a parent's lap, in a coffin or resting peacefully. Adults photographed after death could also be found in a variety of poses. It is not unusual to find a photograph of an open casket in a living room with images of other family members propped up in the casket.

Photographs of the deceased were sometimes incorporated into a tombstone design. Photos on a tombstone are extremely rare, but they do exist.

With the popularity of the card photograph, preprinted black memorial cards became part of the funeral services serving as remembrances of the deceased. Additional copies of photos previously taken could also be ordered and mounted on black card stock or printed with a black border.

Certain compositional elements, such as the inclusion of props, can date a memorial image. For instance, in the 1860s deceased infants were often photographed in their baby carriages.

Death could also be alluded to in a photograph. Individuals holding photographs or wearing jewelry with a photograph as part of it, such as a locket

For More Info

FOR FURTHER DISCUSSION

For a more complete description of postmortem photographs, see *Sleeping Beauty: Memorial Photography in America*, by Stanley Burns, M.D. (Altadena, Calif.: Twelvetrees Press, 1990).

Photographs document all aspects of our ancestor's lifetime. *Lynn Betlock*

or pin, may be an indication of someone not present, either due to death or absence.

Reexamining your family photograph collection can help you gain a sense of the important episodes in your ancestors' lives. The types of images they chose to document can help place them in historical context.

CHECKLIST OF PHOTOGRAPHS USUALLY FOUND IN FAMILY COLLECTIONS

Portraits

- Individuals
- Mother and child
- Family group portrait
- Posed with friends
- Posed in front of dwelling

Children

- Infant portrait
- Mother and child
- Posed with siblings
- Posed with family pet
- Individual portrait

Weddings

- Single portrait of bride and groom
- Double portrait of the couple
- Group portrait of the wedding party
- Photograph of the gifts
- Engagement portrait
- Candid photographs of the event
- Anniversary photo

Military Service

- Portraits of individuals in uniform
- Regimental photographs
- War scenes
- Photo albums of wartime activities
- Photographs of other service personnel

School

- Student portraits
- Class photographs
- Graduation pictures
- Informal photographs of class activities

Holidays and Special Events
- New Year's cards
- Christmas cards
- Parades
- Social activities

Vacations
- Albums and snapshots of activities
- Landmarks visited
- Purchased images of places visited

Postmortem
- Memorial portrait
- Memorial cards
- Tombstone
- Cemetery
- Group portrait with the deceased

EIGHT

Identifying Costume

"Uniforms, fancy dresses, and articles of ladies [sic] attire can be sent to the studio, where dressing rooms, fitted with every convenience, are provided for the use of visitors."

—Coleman and Remington, Photographic Artists, 25 Westminster St., Providence. From the Rhode Island Historical Society

Costume can be useful when dating and interpreting a photograph. A style of hat or the way a woman wears her hair, for instance, can assign a date to an image. **However, you need to be careful when dating clothing.** It is very easy to make a mistake, so always double check your conclusions by looking at other images from the same time period, either in your own collection or in books.

To interpret an image using clothing, you need to be aware of the details in the costume. Not only what is being worn, but how it is worn. **The lack of a particular accessory or the fit of a dress can help you draw conclusions about the wearer.** For example, a portrait of a woman may show that she is wearing parts of two different dresses because the fabric is different in the bodice and skirt. This detail reveals that the woman tried to be fashionable even though economics prevented it.

Costume can also be used to deceive. In some tourist locations, you can have your photograph taken in period clothing. A friend had a tintype of himself taken in a Civil War uniform. Not only was the nineteenth-century process copied, but the clothing as well. In a family photograph collection it would be easy to misidentify both the person and the time period of this image based solely on costume interpretation.

Dressing for a photograph was an important part of having a portrait taken. The images that are in family collections generally show relatives wearing their finest clothing. In order for their patrons to look their best in a studio portrait, some photographers lent clothing and accessories. Popular magazines such as *Godey's Lady's Book* advised women how to dress for portraits.

Important

Tip

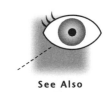

See Also

Appendix E, on page 121, lists magazines to help you date costume and interior photos.

Accessories can help date an image. *Collection of the author*

Children's clothing resembles adult fashions. *Collection of the author*

The basic elements of women's clothing remained the same during the nineteenth and early twentieth century regardless of economic status. A woman's costume consisted of a dress. The details of the garment—the bodice, neckline, sleeves and skirt—help date the dress. Accessories were a necessary part of a well-dressed woman's costume. This could include gloves, jewelry and bonnets or hats. The variety and style of these accessories varied from decade to decade; however, this essential costume remained the same until the early twentieth century.

There was little variation in men's clothing during the same period. The articles of a man's dress outfit consisted of a coat, shirt, trousers, tie, and possibly a vest. The style of men's hats and vests and the color or pattern of the shirt changed over time. Men's work clothes consisted of a collarless shirt, no tie, pants, suspenders and possibly a vest.

Children's clothing for the most part resembled adult dress in the nineteenth and early twentieth century. Babies of both sexes wore long dresses with the length and details dictated by fashion. Toddlers can be seen in essentially the same style of clothing, the length of the dress shortened so that movement could be permitted. Boys wore short pants while girls wore dresses. In photographs where boys and girls are dressed alike, one way to tell them apart is by hairstyle. Girls usually wore their hair parted in the middle and boys parted on the side. Since children's clothing styles changed as they grew older, it is possible to estimate the age of children based on their clothing. For instance, the length of a girl's skirt was relative to her age; a girl's skirt became gradually longer as she approached adulthood.

When you examine your photographs for costume details you may notice that clothing was used to convey a sense of belonging to a group. Sports teams and club group portraits often feature a certain style of clothing. For instance, theatrical performers in the late nineteenth century often sat for portraits to commemorate a play. Group portraits provide clues to activities in which your ancestors took part. The costume of a team may not only help you date the image, but will add additional information to your family history.

Clothing styles also reflected changes within a family. During pregnancy or while working around the house women wore loose dresses called wrappers. Graduation photos of young women show them dressed entirely in white including their shoes. A whole ritual of fashion surrounded mourning. The presence of black crepe on the collars and cuffs of a woman's dress

Tip

Clothing can identify a person's participation in a group. *David Lambert*

indicates she is in mourning. Social conventions merged with fashion, so that the prevalence of black accessories could suggest the length of time a woman was in mourning. Recent widows wore all black, while those in extended mourning could wear white accessories.

Immigrants often abandoned full ethnic dress upon arrival to America in order to look less like newcomers. Occasionally the choice of accessories can identify ethnicity, such as caps, or headscarves like mantillas.

The best guide to fashion in photographs is Joan Severa's *Dressed for the Photographer: Ordinary Americans & Fashion, 1840-1900* **(Kent, Ohio: Kent State University Press, 1995).** The charts on pages 66-70 can be used as a guide for comparing styles of clothing based on the images presented in her book and on lectures presented by Nancy Rexford, a leading costume historian.

Printed Source

WOMEN'S FASHIONS

1840–1847	
Bodice	Long and tight with fan-shaped gathering; pointed in the front; back fastening.
Neckline	Wide, shallow, horizontal neckline gradually gets narrower.
Sleeves	Long, tight to arm, with tight oversleeve on upper arms.
Accessories	Fingerless gloves; gold watches on a long chain; caps, bonnets; ribbon bracelets.
Hair	Large combs; center part; close to head; long ringlets.
1848–1852	
Bodice	Long and tight with fan shape; pointed in the front; could be padded; back fastening.
Neckline	High stand collar.
Sleeves	Three-quarter or long flaring out toward bottom in bell shape worn over white undersleeve.
Accessories	Fingerless gloves; gold watches on a long chain; caps, bonnets; ribbon bracelets.
Hair	Large combs; center part; close to head; spreading over ears.
1853–1860	
Bodice	Front fastening (near middle of decade); some buttons; some jacket-style, flare over skirt.
Neckline	Broad collar; narrower collars at end of period.
Sleeves	Flowing wide at the wrists, worn over white undersleeve; some full sleeves gathered into wristband in less formal dresses.
Skirt	Wider; full, gathered or pleated; some flounces; skirt worn over a hoop by end of the decade.
Accessories	Decoration of dress; ornamental hair jewelry.
Hair	Center part; wide above the ears, then droops over ears.

WOMEN'S FASHIONS (Continued)

1860–1865	
Bodice	Front buttons; pointed or round waists; military trim.
Neckline	High, narrow, round collar, some V necks with lapels.
Sleeves	Armhole over shoulder; some gathered into the wrist; some wide bell; some coat sleeves wider at elbow; variety of styles.
Skirt	Full, pleated, some looped up to expose underskirt; worn over hoop.
Accessories	Shawls, hair nets, wide belts; elaborate earrings and brooches.
Hair	Center part; covers most of ear, plain or braids around; short ringlets.

1866–1868	
Bodice	Front buttons; short waist; slightly raised waistline.
Neckline	High with narrow round or pointed collar; lace or ribbon tie.
Sleeves	Armhole over shoulder; narrower coat sleeve.
Skirt	Broad A-line shape over hoop, few pleats in front.
Accessories	Shawls.
Hair	Center part; pulled tightly back above the ears, piled high in back.

1869–1874	
Bodice	Trim such as ruffles; prominent buttons large, not flat.
Neckline	High with low stand collar or V neck with ruffles.
Sleeves	Armhole over shoulder; wider coat sleeves with cuff effects; moderate bell with trim or ruffles.
Skirt	Trimmed apron-like overskirt with bustle over trimmed underskirt; large bustle.
Accessories	Black velvet neck ribbon with brooch or charm; large lockets and crosses; jet beads; earrings and necklace matched.
Hair	Center part; use of false hair; large hair combs; some hair curled at forehead; long hair streaming down back with hair braided at crown.

1875–1877	
Bodice	Often ruffles around neckline and down front.
Neckline	Front opening, low stand collar; or V neck with ruffles.
Sleeves	Sleeves narrower, still cuff trim.
Skirt	Long overskirt effects, bustle less large; trains common.
Accessories	Large button earrings; large hair combs.
Hair	Center part; frizzed at forehead; braided high at back.

1878–1882	
Bodice	Front buttons; flat, large round or oval buttons; bodice extends over hips.

WOMEN'S FASHIONS (Continued)

Neckline	High with low stand collar.
Sleeves	Sleeves narrower.
Skirt	Fell straight from hip to floor.
Accessories	Fans, parasols.
Hair	Center part; frizzing, low at back.
1883–1889	
Bodice	Tight, waistcoat effects; bodice extends just below the waist.
Neckline	High with low stand collar, fewer lace ties.
Sleeves	Sleeves tight, three-quarter length, trim at bottom.
Skirt	Draped overskirt, often apron-like in shape.
Accessories	Muffs, jewelry.
Hair	Frizzed around forehead; bun in back.
1890–1892	
Bodice	Fastening obscured; ends at or near natural waist.
Neckline	High neck with moderate stand collar.
Sleeves	Tight to arm in 1890 with kick-up at shoulder becoming fuller each year.
Skirt	Drapery gradually smoothes out to stiff columnar shape.
Accessories	Round brooch, small earrings, watch pinned to bosom; large fans, large parasols.
Hair	Frizzed around face; bun on top of head.
1893–1896	
Bodice	Fastening obscured; ruffles over shoulders; gathers in bodice.
Neckline	High collar to chin with bow at side back.
Sleeves	Ruffles, large balloon "leg-o'-mutton" shapes on upper arm; tight below.
Skirt	Smooth at hips, front/sides; gradual flare to stiff A-line effect; sometimes trim at the hem.
Accessories	Feather boa, large fans, parasols.
Hair	Frizzed, curled around face, bun in back.
1897–1900	
Bodice	Asymmetrical, horizontal drapery, blouse-like fullness overhangs waist at center front.
Neckline	High collar to chin, bow at side back of neck.
Sleeves	Decreasing, first small ball-shaped fullness at top, then tight, flaring over hand.

WOMEN'S FASHIONS (Continued)

Skirt	Smooth at hip front/sides; broad A-line becomes slimmer, may flare out below knees.
Accessories	Round brooch, small earrings, watch pinned to bosom; small decorative combs high on back of head visible from front.
Hair	Soft but smoother around face, less frizzing; drawn into back bun.

1901–1903	
Bodice	Pouched front pronounced.
Neckline	High collar to chin.
Sleeves	Fullness increasing year by year on lower arm above cuff only.
Skirt	Smooth at hip front/sides; flares from knee down.
Hair	Soft but smoother around face, less frizzing; drawn into back bun.

1904–1907	
Bodice	Pouched front continues over wider waistbands.
Neckline	High collar to chin; a few collarbone level in summer.
Sleeves	1904: fullness on upper and lower arms; 1905-07: fullness only on upper, sleeves appear to be made in upper and lower sections.
Skirt	Smooth at hips or soft gathers or pleats; generally less slim.
Hair	Gradually gaining width around the face; coiled in back.

1908–1914	
Bodice	Vertical trim effects, small square or round dickey effects; waistline often slightly raised.
Neckline	High collar to chin or round/square to collarbone.
Sleeves	Increasingly tight and plain; some imitate tight lace undersleeves.
Skirt	Increasingly slim, straight, no gathers, feet show.
Hair	Some center parts; puffed out wide at sides to support big hats.

MEN'S FASHIONS

1840–1850	
Coats	Extra-long, narrow sleeves.
Shirt	Dress: tailored white cotton; narrow sleeves; small collar turned up under a tie. Work: colors and patterns or smocks.
Necktie	Tied in a horizontal bowknot, dark-colored.
Trousers	Fly-front.
Hair & Beard	Ear-length, parted high at one side; clean shaven but fringe beards.

MEN'S FASHIONS (Continued)

1850–1860	
Coats	Generous cut; vests.
Shirt	Collar turned over the tie. Work: colors and patterns. Dress: pleated starched bib fronts. Shirt fronts could be purchased.
Necktie	2″ wide, half-bow.
Trousers	Fly-front; wide pant legs.
Hair & Beard	Clean shaven; end of decade full beards appear. Oiled hair, long on top, side part, combed into wave at center of forehead; collar length; ears covered later in the decade.

1860–1870	
Coats	Long, overlarge sack coats.
Shirt	Collars folded down around the neck; white, stripes and plaids.
Necktie	Narrow.
Trousers	Wide, longer at the heel; suspenders common.
Hair & Beard	Chin whiskers; hair at ear level in back; side part.

1870–1880	
Coats	Shorter and close-fitting; narrower; buttoned at top button only to show vest.
Shirt	Made without collars; collars purchased. White, blue, red, black or gray stripes, small plaids.
Necktie	Wide and tied in a loose knot; ends overlap. Striped.
Accessories	Fur hats and coats.

1880–1890	
Coats	Short sacks; narrow sleeves high on shoulder.
Shirt	White.
Necktie	Variety of ties, wide and soft.
Trousers	Narrow with no creases.

1890–1900	
Coats	Narrow, small coats; buttoned all the way to the top.
Shirt	White shirts, trim-fitted collars, small and stiff; toward end of decade collar may be very high and stiff.
Necktie	Black bow tie; narrow ties of black or patterns.
Trousers	Narrow.
Hair & Beard	Short haircuts; large mustaches.

DATING A PHOTOGRAPH USING COSTUME CLUES

There are three steps to using costume to date a photograph. The first step is to carefully examine the photograph and the clothing being worn for any clues. The charts in this chapter (see pages 66-70) outline the major styles that date men and women's clothing. A woman's outfit can be broken down into parts such as the bodice, the shape of the neckline, sleeves and skirt, and the type of accessories being worn. How a woman wore her hair was also an important component of her costume. The shape of the coat, width of the trousers, style of necktie and accessories identify men's clothing.

Step By Step

Once you have made an estimate of the time frame based on the costume clues, consult magazines and store catalogs (see selected list in Appendix E, page 121), and books of published photographs (see Bibliography, page 128) to compare your analysis.

If you are still having problems placing the photograph within a fashion context, you might want to consult a costume professional. Some historical societies and museums have someone on staff who specializes in costume history.

Case Study

CASE STUDY: ALICE McDUFF

Family identifies the photograph of a fashionably dressed young woman on page 72 as Alice McDuff. This image was once in her possession. The family would like to know when the photograph was taken and for what purpose. It is possible that this photograph was taken around the time of her wedding in 1916.

The imprint on this cabinet card identifies the photographer as Harbeck of Pawtucket, Rhode Island. City directory research for Harbeck lists a Jean L. Harbeck of Pawtucket in the photographic business from 1903 to 1940. This does not assign a more specific date to the image.

Upon close examination of the image, the key elements of the outfit are identified: high waist, fitted bodice and skirt, lots of trim and buttons, high neckline and ankle-length skirt. **By consulting John Peacock's *20th Century Fashion* (London: Thames and Hudson, 1993) and comparing the photo to his sketches, a tentative date for the photograph based on costume is 1910-1916.**

Printed Source

The accessories help assign a final date. Alice is wearing a watch pinned to the bodice of her dress and a locket around her neck. A family member owns both pieces of jewelry, but neither one has a date engraved on it. The locket is a friendship token with a picture of Alice and a friend enclosed in the locket. Their initials are engraved on the exterior of the piece. The watch is identified as model Molly Stark manufactured by the Hampden Watch Co. of Canton, Ohio. Alice is wearing this in an earlier family group portrait.

The final key to the mystery can be found in the ring on her left hand.

Family members wanted to know when this portrait was taken. *Alice Taylor*

The photographer posed her so that the ring is a prominent feature of the portrait. It is almost certain that this photograph and one of her husband taken at the same time were a pair of wedding portraits. Alice McDuff and Joseph Bessette were married in 1916. The costume clues and genealogical data support this conclusion.

NINE

Talking With Relatives

"Looking at family photographs makes you remember people and events you had forgotten."

—James W. Taylor, Jr., 18 January 1999

F amily history is the accumulation of information that exists in documents, photographs and memories. Talking with relatives is a necessary part of any family research, but it becomes more important when photographs are involved. By showing the images to family members, you may discover the names and the stories behind the photographs. The process of collecting verbal memories through interviewing is called oral history.

The first step in an oral history interview is to locate family members who

Important

Why was this little girl in the center looking up? This photograph helped her remember the events surrounding this image. *Lynn Betlock*

Idea Generator

SAMPLE INTERVIEW QUESTIONS

Do you recognize the photograph?

When do you think this photo was taken?

Are any of the people in the photograph familiar?

Who are they and how do you know them?

Was this picture taken for a particular occasion?

Does this photograph remind you of any family events or stories?

Who owned the photograph before you?

Do you know who originally owned the photograph?

Do you have a collection of family photographs?

have a sense of family history and can recall it. In some cases, the older members of a family will remember stories, while in others, the younger relatives will be the most helpful. You may want to show the image you are trying to date and interpret to more than one relative. Everyone remembers an event differently; that is, certain details are retained by some individuals better than others are. An elderly relative may remember all the names of the people in the portrait and may also tell you a story about the day the picture was taken. One relative talked about what it had been like to travel to the city to sit for a family portrait. She recalled that she had never seen a tin ceiling before and couldn't take her eyes away from it. Her story explained why she was looking up in the family portrait. She could provide a date for the image, but the story she told about it enriched the family history.

When showing a photograph to relatives, prepare a list of questions prior to your visit.

The photograph will dictate the type of questions you would ask. The details that appear in the image may lead to other avenues of enquiry. A friend showed her much older siblings a box of family photographs in order to find out when and where they were taken. All the images were taken before she was born, so she was unfamiliar with the events and the people. During the course of the interview, the siblings began using nicknames for each other that they had used as children. The younger sibling was amazed. She was unaware of these nicknames, since, her siblings explained, they had only used them to communicate between themselves. Her siblings shared with her the origins of those nicknames and why they used them. A whole new understanding of her immediate family was uncovered in one afternoon by looking at family photographs.

Tip

Photographs offer clues about immigrant experiences. *Collection of the author*

Bring a good quality photocopy of the image with you so that you can leave it with your relative. They may want to consult the photograph again later. A follow-up visit can lead to more discoveries. One family learned of some documents in a distant relative's possession after they showed a relative a few photographs of an ancestor. The documents had become separated from the images in a few generations.

Relatives can also help you decipher captions that appear on the photographs. Captions can include partial names or nicknames of the people depicted. These might refer to "Aunt Eliza" or to "Polly" or tell you that the photograph was a gift "From Tante to Fredy." More complete captions might even include the date the picture was taken and the life dates of the person depicted. On the back of one photograph was "Dear Sister Harriet born Febr.16, 1840—Lee Cor, Penna, Franklin T.P. died Reunion Cor. Penna Oct.1865 New Hope T.P." By interviewing a relative, you may learn the surname of the person mentioned in a similar caption. This additional information will allow you to do more genealogical research on that ancestor.

Until the genealogical research is complete, there is no proof that people in your collection are members of your family. They could be friends of the family. For instance, on the back on one photograph appeared the following caption: "My best girlfriend who I went to school with." Just the presence

Important

Important

These three young men called themselves "The Chieftans." *Lynn Betlock*

of this caption eliminates this image from consideration as a direct family member.

In another image, an extensive caption appeared on the back written in a foreign language. Relatives identified the woman in the image but were unable to translate the message. The owner of this photograph was hopeful that it would reveal family information. When translated, the caption revealed that this was a picture of the woman's new business. She had just opened it and was proud of her accomplishment, including her new telephone. Without the caption, the information in the image would be a puzzle.

Case Study

CASE STUDY: BESSETTE FAMILY

In the casual group portrait on page 77 are several family members and at least one unidentified individual. When the photograph was shown to an older family member, a story was provided. She explained that this was a picture of her parents, herself and an older sibling. She assumed that the one unidentified person in the image must be a boarder, since her family operated a boardinghouse. The two older children in the photograph were cousins that were living with them at the time.

Interviewing relatives is one way to identify images. *Alice Taylor*

According to the narrator, she is the toddler in the image. The young child in the image is her older sister Loretta who was born 25 November 1916 to Eugene Joseph Bessette and his wife Alice (McDuff) who are depicted in the image. The older girl is Dolores. She and her brother, Pete, not depicted, were the children of Albert McDuff, the brother of Alice. They were supposedly living with the Bessettes because their mother had died.

Census records verify the name of the parents and the baby, but do not identify the name of the unknown person or prove that Pete and Dolores were living with the couple. City directories provide an address for the family, but do not offer any evidence that the family operated a boardinghouse. Family folklore and passenger lists confirm that the family traveled between the United States and Canada to visit relatives. In fact, the Bessettes' first child, Loretta, was born in Canada.

By consulting the genealogical data on the McDuff family, it was possible to contact a sibling of Pete and Dolores from their father's second marriage. He filled in a few missing pieces. His father, Albert McDuff, lived with his parents for several years so that they could help him care for his two children after the death of his first wife. In fact, Pete and Dolores never lived with the Bessettes, according to their younger sibling. Alice (McDuff) Bessette, as the youngest member of the McDuff household, was also living at home at the time her brother lived there with the two children. She helped her parents care for the children.

While it was not possible to verify the unknown person in the photo or the boardinghouse story, research was able to help verify the majority of visual family information presented in the image. In this case, oral history interviews helped us interpret the image. They provided the details of the story and the names of the primary subjects. Without this information, it would have been difficult to research the image. While the oral history interviews did not answer all the questions raised by this image, they supported the genealogical research.

TEN

Library Research for Photographs

"A book that is shut is just a block." —Thomas Fuller, *Gnomologia*, No. 23 (1732)

Once you have spoken with other family members, the best place to continue your research is in a library. The purpose of a research trip is to fill in the blanks on your worksheets with data. You may find yourself in an academic library, at a local historical society library, or using the special services offered by a public library. Other types of research assistance can be gathered by using the Internet or by borrowing materials through a lending library. If you have a large collection of photographs to research, you will probably want to start a home library.

Your local public library can be a very helpful first stop. There are at least three areas of the library that may have materials you need. **The reference department, periodical department and the local history collection will all have resources you will want to consult.**

Reference:
- reference books such as costume encyclopedias and antique manuals
- card catalogs
- on-line resources

Periodicals:
- indexes to various magazines and newspapers
- copies of magazines and newspapers

Local history collection:
- photographs, maps and published histories of the area

If you are looking for information outside your local area, the librarians

Sources

Printed Source

may direct you to *The American Library Association Directory of Libraries*. It is primarily an index to libraries in the United States, although it includes material on Canada and Mexico. Each citation provides a brief description of the library including departments, special services and any special collections they maintain. This list includes not just public libraries but private libraries as well.

If you discover that the materials you need are located at another library, a librarian may be able to obtain it via interlibrary loan. Most public libraries and many academic libraries participate in this cooperative loaning arrangement. Occasionally there will be a charge for this service, and there can also be conditions associated with a loan. For instance, the lending library may require that you use the material in the library.

While most public libraries have a local history collection, you may want to visit a special library. An archive or special collection usually refers to an institution or department that collects manuscripts, photographs, books and other materials on a specific subject. Major genealogical libraries fall into the category of special libraries.

Tip

Archives and special libraries have rules for the use of their collections. For example, most archives will require you to place personal materials such as handbags and briefcases in lockers. Generally, you should bring in only the materials you actually need for the research you are currently undertaking. Pencils are required instead of pens. You will also be asked for identification. They may even have you fill out a form asking about the resources that you have already consulted to suggest appropriate materials in their collection.

Printed Source

The National Union Catalog of Manuscript Collections **(NUCMC), published annually, is one important reference tool for locating manuscripts and photographs.** Established in 1959 by the Library of Congress, it offers detailed descriptions of manuscript collections in public, private and academic libraries. They represent abstracts of collections held in at least thirteen hundred different repositories. The collections contain a variety of materials for genealogical researchers including letters, diaries, business papers and photographs. A two-volume cumulative index to personal names is available for volumes published between 1959 and 1984 (Chadwick-Healy, 1988). After 1984 indexes are in the back of each volume. When searching, you should also check for relevant churches, schools, organizations, and other family surnames. Each basic description contains the following information: collection name, repository name, NUCMC number, type of collection, dates, extent and description.

Timesaver

A less time-consuming way to search for manuscripts is to go to a public library or an academic institution to get access to Archives USA. This product, available via the Internet or on CD-ROM, is a combination of all the finding aids submitted for inclusion in the *National Union Catalog of Manuscript Collections* (NUCMC); the *National Inventory Document Survey* (NIDS), a names and subject listing to manuscripts available in a microfiche series;

and the *Directory of Archives and Manuscript Repositories in the United States* (DAMRUS).

Some archives and special collections specialize in historic photographs. **You can find a list of these institutions by consulting the American Library Association's *Directory of Libraries* and the American Museum Association's *Museum Directory*.**

Printed Source

PATENT DEPOSIT LIBRARIES

Another type of special library is a patent deposit facility. When inventors want assurance that their invention will be protected, they register it with the United States Patent Office. These patents are public information and are stored at deposit libraries across the country. **Addresses for patent deposit libraries are listed in Appendix B, page 107.**

Library/Archive Source

Many early photographers patented their improvements to photographic processes. If photographers advertise that they use a particular process, a patent search will help you date the image. Some photographers' imprints include a patent number. Props could also be registered with the patent office. Since each patent contains a drawing of the invention, consulting the

Library/Archive Source

SPECIAL LIBRARIES

George Eastman House
International Museum of Photography
Rochester, NY 14607
http://www.eastman.org
They maintain a library and archive on the history of photography.

United States Army Military History Institute
Attn: Special Collections
22 Ashburn Dr.
Carlisle, PA 17013-5008
http://Carlisle-www.army.mil/usamhi/photoDB.html
Photographs from the Mexican-American War of 1846 to the present are collected. The bulk of the material dates from the Civil War. Represented in the collection are individual portraits and group portraits. Copies can be made for a fee.

Steamship Historical Society of America, Baltimore
University of Baltimore Library
1420 Maryland Ave.
Baltimore, MD 21201
Their photo archives contain more than 50,000 images arranged alphabetically by the name of the ship. Copies can be made for a fee. Research fees will be charged if a request is particularly time-consuming.

Step By Step

patent records may also help date the photograph. **There are two steps to completing a patent search.**

1. Find the subject category that best describes your idea. For patents from 1790 to 1873, you can use the three-volume *Subject Matter Index of Patents for Inventions Issued by the United States Patent Office from 1790 to 1873.* Each volume is alphabetically arranged by invention. The tables also include the name of the inventor, residence, the date of the patent and the number.

2. Look up the patent number in either the *Annual Reports for the Patent Office* for a brief synopsis and a drawing of the invention, or the microfilm copy of the entire patent record.

For instance, by consulting the subject index for photographic chairs you can find one patented by C.G. Pease. This was a special chair for holding sitters still while having their picture taken. By looking at the annual reports of the patent office, published each year and arranged by patent number, you can find an abstract description of the adjustable headrest and a diagram of the device. A look at the full record supplies additional details.

RESEARCH RESOURCES ON-LINE

Internet Source

Not all of your research will be done in a traditional library setting. **There are a variety of materials available on-line that can help you with photo research.** For instance, planning a research trip involves outlining the materials you want to see by subject. Using on-line card catalogs you can create a bibliography of specific books.

Many academic institutions subscribe to databases, encyclopedias and other basic reference tools that will save you a visit to the library. Staff members at academic libraries create research guidelines for specific subjects with on-line addresses. A good research strategy is to consult the on-line card catalog of the largest library in your area to create a bibliography of print and on-line resources.

You can also use your computer to communicate with others via E-mail. It enables you to correspond with collectors, organizations or other family members. For instance, you may discover that a book you have been unable to obtain is still available from an organization specializing in the topic.

Local historical societies are slowly creating Web sites. While the content of these sites varies, they generally tell you how to contact the society, outline their collections and post their hours. Some of the larger historical societies have finding aids for their collections as part of their Web site.

In order to find out what is available in cyberspace, it is best to start with a search engine or a site that indexes other sites on a specific topic. If you search for a specific locality using a standard search engine, you will find material generated on topics ranging from business to education. However, if you consult a Web index created for a specific topic, such as photographs, you will find more information that is relevant to your research.

Internet Source

WEB DIRECTORIES

http://www.cyndislist.com provides links to sites of a genealogical nature.

http://www.city-gallery.com contains articles about the history of photography and links to other sites.

WHAT CAN YOU DO FROM HOME?

There is a tremendous amount of additional research that can be done from home. **There are libraries that will lend books and microfilm to individuals. The National Archives will allow members to borrow microfilm.** For a list of these lending libraries, see the chart on page 84.

Microfilm Source

BUILDING A HOME LIBRARY

If you have a large family photograph collection, you will want to build a home library that you can refer to as needed. Basic volumes include a guide to photographic processes, a general history of photography, an overview of costume history, a genealogical research guide and a printed family genealogy (if one exists). If your photograph collection is comprised of mostly one type of image such as daguerreotypes, you might want to purchase books on that topic as a resource. **A few suggestions for a home library:**

Croom, Emily Anne. *Unpuzzling Your Past: A Basic Guide to Genealogy.* 3rd ed. Cincinnati, Ohio: Betterway Books, 1995.

Mace, O. Henry. *Collector's Guide to Early Photographs.* Radnor, Pa.: Wallace-Homestead Book Co., 1990.

Reilly, James M. *Care and Identification of 19th Century Photographic Prints.* Rochester, N.Y.: Eastman Kodak, 1986.

Rose, Christine, and Kay Germain Ingalls. *The Complete Idiot's Guide to Genealogy.* New York: Alpha Books, 1997.

Severa, Joan. *Dressed for the Photographer: Ordinary Americans and Fashion, 1840-1900.* Kent, Ohio: Kent State University Press, 1995.

Tuttle, Craig A. *An Ounce of Preservation: A Guide to Care of Papers and Photographs.* Highland City, Fla.: Rainbow Books, 1995.

A basic set of reference books can save you countless trips to the library. If you have a sizable collection or are trying to construct one, assembling a home library is a worthwhile investment.

Printed Source

Research Tip

Library/Archive Source

LENDING LIBRARIES

National Genealogical Society
4527 Seventeenth St. North
Arlington, VA 22207-2399
(703) 525-0050 or (800) 473-0060
http://www.ngsgenealogy.org
Members can borrow books from their library.

New England Historic Genealogical Society
101 Newbury St.
Boston, MA 02116
(617) 536-5740
http://www.nehgs.org
The Society maintains a separate Circulating Library for members.

National Archives (NARA)
Pennsylvannia Ave. at Eighth St., N.W.
Washington, DC 20408
(800) 788-6282
http://www.nara.gov
A select list of microfilms of material in the National Archives can be borrowed directly from them.

American Genealogical Lending Library
P.O. Box 329
Bountiful, UT 84011-0329
(800) 760-2455 ext. 523
http://www.agll.com
Members of their Research Club can borrow microfilm and microfiche.

ELEVEN

Building a Family Collection

"With a daguerreotype likeness, I will with pleasure furnish you quite soon to be placed in your domestic Museum of the Cushmans."

—Letter from Benjamin Cushman to Henry Wyles Cushman, 1853. From the Cushman Collection, New England Historic Genealogical Society

Now that you have researched the photographs in your collection, you may want to locate additional images. **The best source of pictures is the collections of other relatives.** Some of the other sources for family photographs are newspapers, archives, publications and naturalization papers. You can even find photographs by searching the Web.

There are several basic steps in building a family photograph collection:
1. Create a list of all ancestors that may have had their photograph taken.
2. Reexamine all available documents for information.
3. Contact all living relatives.
4. Search for all possible sources of photographs.
5. Caption all the images for the future.

A preliminary approach to finding photographs is to make a list of all family members and ancestors that might exist in photographs. This list would include anyone living from 1839 to the present. This family timeline helps organize your search.

The first step in locating photographs is to reexamine all the family documents already in your possession. An immigrant ancestor's naturalization papers may have a photograph. Even marriage certificates may include photographs. For instance, in the late nineteenth century commercial publishers offered printed marriage certificates, memorial certificates and even family tree charts for sale. These included spaces for photographs.

Sources

Step By Step

Sources

SOURCES OF FAMILY PHOTOGRAPHS

Relatives	Passports
Family friends	Mug books
Licenses	Criminal records
Work passes	Family genealogies
Health records	Marriage certificates
School and college yearbooks	Memorial certificates
Newspapers	Family tree templates
Naturalization papers	Manuscript collections

The next step is to contact other relatives. In order to locate the rest of the family photo archive, it will be necessary to reach out to relatives you know and to track down those you don't. Contact the relatives whom you see regularly and ask about photographs. In one family, images surfaced when one of the younger cousins decided to compile a genealogy for the eldest member of the family. The photographs, chronicling several generations, had been in a closet until the cousin asked about them.

Your search should include all living members of the family. Identify all family members who might possess family photographs.

When contacting relatives whom you don't know personally, write them a letter outlining the purpose of your project. You can enclose a question-

Place your ancestors in context by locating a picture of their hometown. *Collection of the author*

naire regarding the types of photographs in their collection. The initial communication should reassure them about the purpose of your query. If you ask for photocopies, offer to pay for them.

PLAN A FAMILY REUNION

In order to contact relatives all at one time, you might want to think about having a family reunion. It can be as formal or informal as you like, but planning is key to success. Outline the purpose of the reunion, pick a date, and select a location. Ask attendees to bring photographs with them.

Research Tip

Reunions Magazine publishes a workbook to help individuals plan such an event. It provides worksheets to help organize a gathering, such as budget sheets and timetables. If most of your family lives in the local area, you might want to plan a scaled-down version.

Reunions **and other family reunion planners suggest a few tips for a successful event:**

Tip

- Talk with others who have already planned a reunion to find out what they would and wouldn't do again.
- Enlist other family members to help with the event.
- Decide on a budget and stick with it.

A family reunion encourages participants to talk about their photographs. You will want to issue a set of guidelines for the types of photos attendees should bring with them. The purpose of the party, besides serving a social function, will be to identify and uncover new family images.

Start the party with a series of activities, such as providing name tags with a photocopy of a picture of the person as a baby or small child. Ask relatives to help supply the images for the name tags.

Set up a mystery photo area for all those unidentified pictures. To avoid damage to the originals, try not to display them in this area. Laser copies, available at most copy shops, or good photocopies should suffice. They can be attached to a bulletin board without concern for damage.

Don't forget to keep a record of the event itself. Ask members of the reunion to be the photographers for the event and create something that will become part of the family photo archive. Supply disposable cameras and make a scrapbook of the event. The availability of digital photo processing will allow you to E-mail copies to attendees.

Reminder

In order to keep a copy of the images that are brought to the reunion, you will want to have access to a photocopy machine that produces good-quality copies of photographs. Look for one with adjustable exposure control from dark to light. Attach a worksheet to each copy to record information about the picture, including the owner's name. If someone in your family is computer savvy, you might want to set up a computer and a scanner to record the images. Have an ample supply of cotton gloves and magnifying glasses available for examining the images.

You may discover that a member of the family will volunteer to be the

Tip

Reminder

Sources

family historian and help you with the task of sorting out all the images. **Be sure to have contributors put their name and address on each of the photocopies to ensure their return.** If several people express an interest, you could create a family preservation committee.

Looking at photographs will encourage relatives to tell stories. Have a tape recorder or camcorder on hand to record these moments.

FRIENDS AND PRINTED SOURCES

After seeking out photograph collections belonging to relatives, try family friends. They can be a good resource, especially for the more recent generations. They may have photographs of events that your relatives attended.

A good way to locate images is to think about the documents that your family members would have created during their lifetimes. Licenses for either work or driving exist for the twentieth century. There are probably not many of us who would want to be remembered by the portrait found on our driver's license, but it is a viable source of pictures. Work passes or identification badges can also contain small pictures.

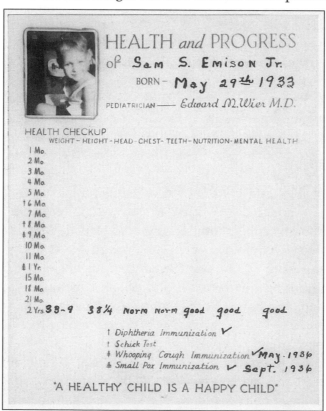

One family collection included a photographic record of each yearly checkup. *Grant Emison*

School photographs, such as class portraits or individual graduation photos, may exist. Yearbooks often included an individual portrait of each student. You may also find your relative in a group portrait representing a school club or team. Some school districts also required a photograph be placed in a student file.

Newspapers generally require an extensive search unless you have specific dates of events. Photographs can sometimes accompany an engagement announcement, a wedding notice or an obituary. For an obituary it is always best to look at seven days' worth of newspapers because it can take awhile for it to appear in print. If at first you don't find the obituary you are looking for, don't forget to check the news items in case the death was related to another event. If you are searching a local newspaper from a small town, you might find pictures related to anniversary celebrations or class reunions, in advertisements, or on the society page.

Professional journals may also have featured your relative in an article along with a photograph. Regional magazines often focus on local events or personalities. You could be lucky and find a candid of a relative partying at an event. Most newspapers and magazines maintain an archive of photographs that appeared in print. You may be able to order copies.

Some types of immigration records for obtaining citizenship required photographs. Alien registration cards, also known as green cards, contain a photograph, as do some naturalization papers. In 1929, declarations of intentions included a photograph of the petitioner. Certificates of residence and visas for the late nineteenth through the twentieth century are also good sources of photographs.

Include photographs of your ancestors' gravestones in your collection. *Collection of the author*

Prison records and other types of materials such as court records and police files can be illustrated with photographs. Contact the police department or local courthouse where a crime took place to see if they know the whereabouts of the records.

Local histories or biographical encyclopedias might contain a photograph or illustration of relatives if they were important members of their community. The purpose of the biographical encyclopedias or mug books was to focus on the contributions of the members of a community. An engraving or photograph might appear with the biography. Mug books were often published for special occasions, such as centennials, by vanity presses who would approach the group or organization.

ON-LINE SOURCES

On-line resources should not be overlooked. There are several sites that specialize in helping people locate family collections. The materials that are posted on the sites have been found at auctions and flea markets. Other sites ask for help in identifying images in family collections.

Internet Source

WEB SITES OF INTEREST

Ancestor's Lost and Found
http://www.rootsweb.com/~neresour/ancestors/index.html

Ancestral Photos
http://pwl.netcom.com/~cityslic/photos.htm

PhotoFind Database
http://www.everton.com/photofind

Fallen Leaves
http://www.agcig.org/leaves.htm

Henry Wyles Cushman, a Massachusetts politician, is a good example of a nineteenth-century collector of family photographs. In the 1850s he decided to publish an illustrated genealogy of his family. His intent was to document the contributions of the Cushmans to the history of the United States. He began the process by contacting each living relative to accumulate information and images. In each letter he sent to family members, Cushman asked for a daguerreotype portrait of the person. Some individuals declined, but many consented. In the process of compiling his genealogy, Cushman inadvertently created a family photo archive. It is still in existence today.

LABELING YOUR IMAGES

Important

Now that you have created a family archive, it is important to label each image. A worksheet is a useful tool, but if it becomes separated from the item, the information is lost. The best way to include identification data is to place the photograph in an archival sleeve with a sheet of acid-free paper. Archival materials will not harm your images. You can then write the caption on the acid-free paper with a pencil. Archival-quality materials can be purchased in a local photography store or from a specialty supplier. There is a list in Appendix B, page 103. Acid-free paper can be purchased at most office supply stores.

You can also create an album of your family images, as long as the materials you use are guaranteed safe for photographs. **Albums that use static electricity, glue or plastic overlay to hold the images in place are not safe to use.** Static electricity can damage the picture's surface. Glue will adhere to the picture and can either make it hard to remove the image from the album or bleed through the image. Plastic gives off a gas that over time will damage the surface of the picture. It is best to purchase quality materials from one of the suppliers listed in Appendix B.

Warning

Sample Photo Captions

Any captions that appear on the photograph itself should be placed in quotations.

Person
- Full name, dates of birth and death.
- Name of photographer, date image was taken.
- Event depicted.
- Caption.
- Original owner or citation of where found.

Place
- Geographic location, title of image. If you supply a caption, place it in brackets.
- Name of photographer, date taken.
- Caption information, such as what is depicted.
- Original owner or citation of where found.

Most family albums include images of the family pets.
New England Historic Genealogical Society

TWELVE

Putting All the Clues Together: Two Case Studies

"I've learned so much about my family from photographs." —Jonathan Galli, 12 April 1999

T
he process of interpreting and identifying family images is the same whether you choose to research a single image or a whole collection. The basic steps of examining the image and researching the clues remain the same. In the end, the information you gathered will help you draw conclusions about the photographs.

Two individuals, both experienced genealogists, have spent a great deal of time working with their family photographs. Jonathan Galli, a professional genealogist, has been researching his family and building a family photo archive for about twenty years. Lynn Betlock, however, has spent time researching a particular image from her collection. In both these cases, the research steps begin with studying the image and end with the evaluation.

CASE STUDY: GALLI/MUNN/RICHARDS FAMILY PHOTOGRAPH COLLECTION

The Galli/Munn/Richards photograph collection contains about two hundred images dating from the 1840s to the present. The collection spans the history of photography. There are only a few daguerreotypes, ambrotypes and tintypes, but there is a vast number of images from the later half of the nineteenth century forward.

The first stage of the evaluative process for a collection is to lay out the images in terms of identified family groups and try to establish photographic

Case Study

Tip

School photographs are a prominent part of the Galli family photograph collection. *Jonathan Galli*

timelines for those people. This will establish that (1) there are no images of some family members; (2) there are some misidentified photos; and (3) the images fall into distinct categories.

Most of the images in the Galli/Munn/Richards family archive fall into four categories: school photographs, babies, homes and businesses. There is a small assortment of school photographs that date from the 1880s to the present. There are group portraits of students in a classroom as well as

Family members collected photographs of the houses in which they lived. *Jonathan Galli*

single graduation portraits. Each generation purchased images to memorialize their school experiences.

While there are not a large number of baby photos, there are two small albums that suggest the place of a baby in the family. Each album depicts a baby being held by different paternal family members. Both albums contain images of the paternal side of the family holding a baby. It is possible that these albums were given as gifts since they are so family specific. It is possible that a member of the paternal side of the family created a separate album for each of the couple's two children. The genealogical data shows that several couples in each generation did not have children. The babies in this family were truly a blessed event.

The largest group of images is a group of photographs of various members of the Richards family posed with their houses. Their father was Rev. Thomas Cole Richards. At first glance these images appear to be just houses that different families lived in; however, family stories and genealogical research provide a different meaning. Rev. Richards held pastorates in at least six churches in Massachusetts and Connecticut. It appears that in each new setting, he either took the photo or had one commissioned of his family posed with the house. Unfortunately, no one ever wrote the name of the town or the location of the dwellings on the images, so they remain anonymous.

Several members of the family operated their own businesses. *Jonathan Galli*

The Galli/Munn/Richards family was proud of their accomplishments. Their photograph collection contains images of the family businesses. The Richards' businesses are represented in several images. They document the problems and successes of the family business. The collection includes an image of the mill the family operated in West Winsted, Connecticut. In another photograph there is a sign in front of a pile of rubble that says, "Down and Out/at 502/Up and Doing/ at 715 Main St./Geo. Richards & Son." It documents a fire that destroyed one of their businesses. A third image, on page 94, is a photograph of the truck used for the business, with painted signage on its side.

Most of the nineteenth- and early-twentieth-century pictures are of the Richards family, in particular Louise (Richards) Sherwood (1899-1969). She was an attractive and fashionable young woman who attended the Sorbonne in Paris. Louise obviously liked being photographed, because there are images of her from infancy through adulthood. She was comfortable both in front of the camera as well as behind it. In every family there is someone who becomes the family photographer. In the Richards family, it was Louise. She appears in a family group portrait holding a camera.

Tip

The absence of photographs of individual family members can also tell a story. The majority of pictures are of the Richards family, but there is a noticeable lack of images of A.A. Richards, the progenitor of the family. There is a lovely set of cyanotype images, however, of A.A. Richards, his wife and two daughters. Their costume tells us that they were taken on the same day. The absence of foliage and the way they are attired suggests the images were taken in the spring. An approximate date can be assigned to these images simply by evaluating them in terms of the genealogical data. The baby in the pictures is Eleanor Spencer (Richards) Koonz, who was born in May of 1911. Since she appears to be approximately one year old and other details tell us it is spring, it is possible the pictures were taken in March or April of 1912. This small collection of happy family scenes are the last images of A.A. Richards. He died 25 April 1912.

Misidentified Images

As a genealogist, Jonathan realized the value of his family images and tried to date them using a variety of techniques, such as comparing them for family resemblances, placing the images in the context of genealogical information, and interviewing family members about the images. When he reexamined the collection, it became apparent that a portrait had been misidentified. The photographer was not identified on the image, so no appropriate date could be assigned from that information. He assumed it was Mary (Sparks) Munn who died in 1852; however, the costume clues definitely place the image in the 1870s. When all the pictures of that generation were laid out, it became apparent that there were a series of portraits taken at the same time of different members of the Munn family. All the images are mounted in identical paper frames and the individuals are posed in the same way.

By assessing the costume clues and comparing the genealogical date, Jonathan concluded that the portrait of the woman is probably Mary (Sparks) Munn's daughter, Mary Louise Munn. If that is true, then the man in the series of portraits is her father, and the identity of the young woman is

This photograph was misidentified. *Jonathan Galli*

unknown. It is possible that the younger woman is Mary's sister, but no
data exists to support this theory.

Building the Collection

The Galli/Munn/Richards collection did not exist as a group until Jonathan
Galli began researching his family. As he met and interviewed family members for genealogical material, he began finding photographs that were being
abandoned. The process he used in compiling these images is an illustration
of how to accumulate a photograph collection. The genealogical chart on
page 97 shows who is represented in the collection and who owned the
photographs before Jonathan.

In the course of his research, Jonathan became aware of three collections
from estates with no direct heirs. In these cases, the direct lines had died out.

One particular collection of images was residing with distant relatives.
The story is that a daughter went to live with cousins in New York City for
a short period of time. When she moved back to Dutchess County, New
York, she left the family photographs with her second cousins. By tracking
down the family, Jonathan obtained copy prints but not the originals.

A collection like the Galli/Munn/Richards photographs is not static. Fam-

Galli/Munn/Richards Collection

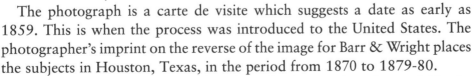

Diodate Theodorus Munn

- Rhoda m. Upson
  - Ellen m. Andrews
  - Belle m. Bates
    - Howard

- Sedusky (1811-1882) m. Mary Sparks (1818-1852)
  - Mary Louise (1839-1919) m. Charles Tyrell (1822-1899)
    - Louise Carrie (b.1865)
    - Eugenia (b.1972)
    - **Ruth Ethel m. Richards**
  - **Emma (b.1847) m. Remer**
    - Helen (b.1906) m. Atwood
      - **Beth Spencer**
      - **Judith Fenn**
    - Eleanor m. Koonz
      - Eleanor m. Galli
        - Jonathan

Key: Shaded boxes show provenance of photographs. Bold identifies subjects represented in photograph collection.

ily photographs accumulate over time and in many different ways. New photographs are added for each generation and become a visual family tree. **It is important to continue to add to your family collection so that future generations can envision what life was like for their ancestors.**

Important

Case Study

CASE STUDY: A FAMILY PHOTO MYSTERY REMAINS

In the Emison/Loock family photo collection is a haunting image of two girls in plaid dresses. Their identity remains a mystery, but the truly elusive fact is an explanation for their bald heads and lack of eyebrows. Lynn Betlock has made several attempts to discover who these mysterious girls are in her husband's family and the reasons for their appearance. Sometimes, even with persistence and patience, images in your collection will defy your efforts to identify them.

The photograph is a carte de visite which suggests a date as early as 1859. This is when the process was introduced to the United States. The photographer's imprint on the reverse of the image for Barr & Wright places the subjects in Houston, Texas, in the period from 1870 to 1879-80.

A costume historian verified that the girls' dresses place them within the 1870s. The historian offered a hint that individuals contracted yellow fever often lost their hair or had their heads shaved.

Library research confirms that there was a major yellow fever epidemic

Several attempts have been made to identify these two girls. *Grant Emison*

in Houston in 1867. In a town of less than 5,000 people 492 people died. Unfortunately, further research refutes the theory that yellow fever was related to the girls' appearance. By consulting the Library of the National Institute of Health's History of Medicine, Lynn was able to learn that only one disease causes hair loss of the type depicted in the photograph. It is alopecia, a congenital condition that causes individuals with it to lose the hair on their bodies.

The Emison family is fairly well documented in photographs from the first decade of the twentieth century to the present, but no photos in the family archive exist for the time period of the girls in the plaid dresses. There is no photographic evidence in the family collection to suggest that alopecia is present.

Genealogical research was the last option. Since the girls appear to be just a few years apart in age, the family history was examined to find a pair of sisters living in Houston in the appropriate time period. The facial resemblance suggests that they are sisters. Unfortunately, there is no caption on the photograph to confirm this relationship. There are also no other photographs of this time period in the Emison family collection to support the conclusion through comparison.

The Loock family became the focus of this research because the photos in the Emison/Loock collection are primarily of the Loock side of the family and were passed to the current generation by a Loock member. Lynn traced several family groups to try to identify these girls, but in each case the genealogical research did not establish an identity for them. The family tree shows the family members that Lynn researched.

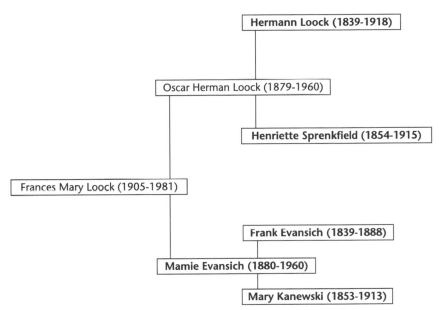

Key: Bold = Families who were considered possibly related to girls.

By comparing the family information with what is known about the image, Lynn considered that two possible individuals were Mamie Evansich and her sister Lula. Research showed that they could not be the girls, however, because they weren't living in Houston in the 1870s. Both girls were born in Brenham, Texas, and Brenham is eighty miles from Houston. More importantly, Mamie and Lula were born too late to be possibilities.

Lynn then tried to locate other Loocks living in the area in the 1870s. Since Loock is such an unusual name, it is possible that any other Loocks living in Houston might be related. In the 1870 census she found another Loock family living in Houston. The daughters of Henrietta Loock Gastman and her husband Henry were approximately the right age. In the 1870 census Henrietta and her husband are twenty-five and thirty respectively. They have three daughters: Dorothea, age 9; Anna, age 7; and Mary, age 4. Any two of these daughters are possibly the subjects of the photograph. Mary is known to have lived to adulthood, but nothing is known about the other two siblings. Unfortunately, no relationship with the other Loock family could be established. The families attended different churches and were not mentioned in baptismal sponsorships and obituaries.

Hermann Loock was born in Hanover, Germany, and was living in Houston in 1870. Once again, however, research showed that not only were his children born too late, but they were both boys.

Another possibility is that the girls' photo found its way into the family collection through family friends. According to the 1870 Texas census, Hermann Loock was living with another family, the Kothmanns, as a boarder. The Kothmanns had two girls that were the right age, but there is no corroborating evidence, such as other images of them, to support this conclusion. There are also no death records for their daughters, so there is no evidence that they were living from 1870 to 1879-80.

All the genealogical research implies that the girls were probably not related to the Loocks. The medical information concerning their lack of hair supports the genetic disease alopecia. No other members of the Loock family have been known to have the disease.

Cartes de visite were collected by nineteenth-century families for a variety of reasons. Medical anomalies were photographed and the images sold to collectors. It is possible that this image falls into that category.

As Lynn Betlock discovered, researching family photographs is a fascinating pursuit because it adds depth to your genealogical research. In family research, you often uncover unexpected information. Photo research helps you discover a few unknown ancestors and put a name with a face.

Timeline of Photographic History

1834	William Henry Fox Talbot announces his paper photographic process to the Royal Society of London.
1839	A patent is issued to Louis Daguerre for a method of capturing images on metal.
1840	Francois Gouraud visits America and demonstrates the daguerreotype process.
	• The first daguerreotype studio opens in New York City.
	• The first school photograph is taken by Samuel F.B. Morse of the Yale Class of 1810.
1842	Patent for coloring daguerreotypes issued to B.F. Stevens and L. Morse.
	• The cyanotype process is announced.
1850	Mathew Brady publishes his *Gallery of Illustrious Americans*. It contains portraits and biographies of eminent American citizens.
	• 1850 census lists 938 males over the age of 15 with the occupation of daguerreotypist.
	• The Langenheim Brothers of Philadelphia commercially introduce stereoscopic views.
1851	Wet plate or wet-collodion negative process is introduced.
1853	Tintype introduced by Hamilton L. Smith of Ohio.
1854	James Ambrose Cutting is issued a patent for the ambrotype.
1856	Alexander Gardner introduces a process for making photographic enlargements.
1857	The Duke of Parma introduces the carte de visite.
1859	Cartes de visite are brought to America.
1860	The carte de visite is mentioned in an ad in *Leslie's Weekly* by S.A. Holmes.
	• First aerial photograph is taken in Boston.
	• Tintype used as a campaign medal for first time.
1861	First patent issued for a photograph album.
	• Amateur Photographic Exchange Club formed.
1864	Marcus A. Root publishes *The Camera and the Pencil*, the first history of American photography.
1864-1866	Revenue stamps are required for photographs.
1868	Photographic retouching is available.
	• H.M. Crider introduces photographic marriage certificates.
1869	Celluoid film, a combination of collodion and camphor, becomes available. This is the beginning of low-cost roll film.
1884	Flash photography using magnesium light introduced.
1888	Kodak roll-film camera introduced with slogan, "You push the button—We do the rest."

1907	Lumiere Brothers invent the Autochrome process.
1914	Kodak issues the No.1 Autographic Kodak Jr. which allows photographer to write date, name and place on film. Made until 1934.
1935	Eastman Kodak introduces Kodachrome low-cost color photography slides and prints.
1947	Edwin H. Land announces a one-step photo process that develops in less than a minute.
1957	Edwin H. Land announces full-color Polaroid pictures.
1963	Kodak issues the Instamatic. Sold 7.5 million in 2 years and 70 million in 10 years.
1972	Polaroid introduces the SX-70.
1991	Kodak makes photo CDs available.

Important Addresses

Conservators

Conservation Center for Art & Historic Artifacts (CCAHA)
264 S. Twenty-third St.
Philadelphia, PA 19103
Phone: (215) 545-0613

Northeast Document Conservation Center (NEDCC)
100 Brickstone Square
Andover, MA 01810
Phone: (508) 470-1010

Ocker & Trapp
17 C Palisade Ave.
Emerson, NJ 07630-0229

National Archives Regional Addresses

Alaska

Anchorage

NARA's Pacific Alaska Region
654 W. Third Ave.
Anchorage, AK 99501-2145
Phone: (907) 271-2443
Fax: (907) 271-2442
E-mail: archives@alaska.nara.gov

California

Laguna Niguel

NARA's Pacific Region
24000 Avila Rd., First Floor-East Entrance
Laguna Niguel, CA 92677-3497
Phone: (949) 360-2641
Fax: (949) 360-2624
E-mail: center@laguna.nara.gov

San Francisco (San Bruno)

NARA's Pacific Region
1000 Commodore Dr.
San Bruno, CA 94066-2350
Phone: (650) 876-9009
Fax: (650) 876-9233
E-mail: center@sanbruno.nara.gov

Sources

Library/Archive Source

Colorado
Denver
NARA's Rocky Mountain Region
   Building 48, Denver Federal Center
   Denver, CO 80225
   P.O. Box 25307
   Denver, CO 80225-0307
   Phone: (303) 236-0804
   Fax: (303) 236-9297
   E-mail: center@denver.nara.gov

Georgia
Atlanta (East Point)
NARA's Southeast Region
   1557 St. Joseph Ave.
   East Point, GA 30344-2593
   Phone: (404) 763-7477
   Fax: (404) 763-7059
   E-mail: archives@atlanta.nara.gov

Illinois
Chicago
NARA's Great Lakes Region
   7358 S. Pulaski Rd.
   Chicago, IL 60629-5898
   Phone: (773) 581-7816
   Fax: (312) 353-1294
   E-mail: archives@chicago.nara.gov

Maryland
Suitland
Washington National Records Center
   4205 Suitland Rd.
   Suitland, MD 20746-8001
   Phone: (301) 457-7000
   Fax: (301) 457-7117
   E-mail: center@suitland.nara.gov

Massachusetts
Boston (Waltham)
NARA's Northeast Region (Boston)
   380 Trapelo Rd.
   Waltham, MA 02452-6399
   Phone: (781) 647-8100
   Fax: (781) 647-8460
   E-mail: archives@waltham.nara.gov

Pittsfield

NARA's Northeast Region (Pittsfield)
  10 Conte Dr.
  Pittsfield, MA 01201-8230
  Phone: (413) 445-6885
  Fax: (413) 445-7599
  E-mail: archives@pittsfield.nara.gov

Missouri

Kansas City

NARA's Central Plains Region (Kansas City)
  2312 E. Bannister Rd.
  Kansas City, MO 64131-3011
  Phone: (816) 926-6272
  Fax: (816) 926-6982
  E-mail: archives@kansascity.nara.gov

Lee's Summit

NARA's Central Plains Region (Lee's Summit)
  200 Space Center Dr.
  Lee's Summit, MO 64064-1182
  Phone: (816) 478-7079
  Fax: (816) 478-7625

St. Louis

NARA's National Personnel Records Center
  Civilian Personnel Records
  111 Winnebago St.
  St. Louis, MO 63118-4199
  Fax: (314) 425-5719
  E-mail: center@cpr.nara.gov
NARA's National Personnel Records Center
  Military Personnel Records
  9700 Page Ave.
  St. Louis, MO 63132-5100
  Fax: (314) 538-4175
  E-mail: center@stlouis.nara.gov

New York

New York City

NARA's Northeast Region (New York City)
  201 Varick St.
  New York, NY 10014-4811
  Phone: (212) 337-1300
  Fax: (212) 337-1306
  E-mail: archives@newyork.nara.gov

Ohio
Dayton
NARA's Great Lakes Region
  3150 Springboro Rd.
  Dayton, OH 45439-1883
  Phone: (937) 225-2852
  Fax: (937) 225-7236
  E-mail: center@dayton.nara.gov

Pennsylvania
Philadelphia
NARA's Mid-Atlantic Region (Center City Philadelphia)
  900 Market St.
  Philadelphia, PA 19107-4292
  Phone: (215) 597-3000
  Fax: (215) 597-2303
  E-mail: archives@philarch.nara.gov
NARA's Mid-Atlantic Region (Northeast Philadelphia)
  14700 Townsend Rd.
  Philadelphia, PA 19154-1096
  Phone: (215) 671-9027
  Fax: (215) 671-8001
  E-mail: center@philfrc.nara.gov

Texas
Fort Worth
NARA's Southwest Region
  501 W. Felix St., Building 1
  Fort Worth, TX 76115-3405
  P. O. Box 6216
  Fort Worth, TX 76115-0216
  Phone: (817) 334-5525
  Fax: (817) 334-5621
  E-mail: archives@ftworth.nara.gov

Washington
Seattle
NARA's Pacific Alaska Region
  6125 Sand Point Way NE
  Seattle, WA 98115-7999
  Phone: (206) 526-6507
  Fax: (206) 526-4344
  E-mail: archives@seattle.nara.gov

Patent Deposit Libraries

Library/Archive Source

Alabama
Ralph Brown Draughon Library
  Auburn University
  231 Mell St.
  Auburn University, AL 36849-5606
  Phone: (334) 844-1747
Birmingham Public Library
  2100 Park Pl.
  Birmingham, AL 35203
  Phone: (205) 226-3620

Alaska
Z.J. Loussac Public Library
  Anchorage Municipal Libraries
  3600 Denali
  Anchorage, AK 99503-6093
  Phone: (907) 562-7323

Arizona
Daniel E. Noble Science and Engineering Library
  Arizona State University
  Tempe, AZ 85287-1006
  Phone: (602) 965-7010

Arkansas
Arkansas State Library
  Dept. of Education
  1 Capitol Mall
  Little Rock, AR 72201-1081
  Phone: (501) 682-2053

California
Los Angeles Public Library
  630 W. Fifth St.
  Los Angeles, CA 90071
  Phone: (213) 228-7220
California State Library
  900 N. St., Room 200
  Sacramento, CA 95814
  Phone: (916) 654-0069
San Diego Public Library
  820 E St.
  San Diego, CA 92101
  Phone: (619) 236-5813

San Francisco Public Library
   Civic Center
   San Francisco, CA 94132-1719
   Phone: (415) 557-4500
Sunnyvale Center for Innovation, Invention & Ideas
   465 South Mathilda Ave., Suite 300
   Sunnyvale, CA 94086
   Phone: (408) 730-7290

Colorado
Denver Public Library
   10 W. Fourteeth Ave. Parkway
   Denver, CO 80204-2731
   Phone: (303) 640-6220

Connecticut
Hartford Public Library
   500 Main St.
   Hartford, CT 06103
   Phone: (860) 543-8628
New Haven Free Public Library
   133 Elm St.
   New Haven, CT 06510-2033
   Phone: (203) 946-8130

Delaware
University of Delaware Library
   Morris Library
   South College Ave. (Route 896)
   Newark, DE 19717-5267
   Phone: (302) 831-2965

District of Columbia
Founders Library
   Howard University
   500 Howard Place NW
   Washington, DC 20059
   Phone: (202) 806-7252

Florida
Broward County Main Library
   100 S. Andrews Ave.
   Fort Lauderdale, FL 33301
   Phone: (954) 357-7444
Miami-Dade Public Library
   101 W. Flagler St.

Miami, FL 33130-1523
Phone: (305) 375-2665
University of Central Florida Library
P.O. Box 162666
Orlando, FL 32816-2666
Phone: (407) 823-2562
Tampa Campus Library
University of South Florida
4202 E. Fowler Ave.
Tampa, FL 33620-5400
Phone: (813) 974-2726

Georgia

Library and Information Center
Georgia Institute of Technology
Atlanta, GA 30332-0900
Phone: (404) 894-4508

Hawaii

Hawaii State Library
478 S. King St.
Honolulu, HI 96813-2901
Phone: (808) 586-3477

Idaho

University of Idaho Library
Rayburn St.
Moscow, ID 83844-2351
Phone: (208) 885-6235

Illinois

Chicago Public Library
9N-15 400 S. State St.
Chicago, IL 60605-1203
Phone: (312) 747-4450
Illinois State Library
300 S. Second St.
Springfield, IL 62701-1796
Phone: (217) 782-5659

Indiana

Indianapolis-Marion County Public Library
40 E. Saint Clair
Indianapolis, IN 46204
Phone: (317) 269-1741
Siegesmund Engineering Library

Purdue University
Potter Center, Room 160
West Lafayette, IN 47907-1250
Phone: (317) 494-2872

Iowa
State Library of Iowa
E. 12th and Grand Sts.
Des Moines, IA 50319
Phone: (515) 281-4118

Kansas
Ablah Library
Wichita State University
Wichita, KS 67260-0068
Phone: (316) 978-3155

Kentucky
Louisville Free Public Library
Fourth and York Sts.
Louisville, KY 40203
Phone: (502) 574-1611

Louisiana
Troy H. Middleton Library
Louisiana State University
Baton Rouge, LA 70803-3300
Phone: (504) 388-8875

Maine
Raymond H. Fogler Library
University of Maine
P.O. Box 5729
Orono, ME 04469-5729
Phone: (207) 581-1678

Maryland
Engineering and Physical Sciences Library
University of Maryland
College Park, MD 20742
Phone: (301) 405-9157

Massachusetts
Physical Sciences and Engineering Library
Lederle Graduate Research Center
University of Massachusetts

Amherst, MA 01003
Phone: (413) 545-1370
Boston Public Library
700 Boylston St.
P.O. Box 286
Boston, MA 02117
Phone: (617) 536-5400 ext. 265

Michigan
Media Union Library
The University of Michigan
1100 Dow
Ann Arbor, MI 48109-2136
Phone: (313) 647-5735
Abigail S. Timme Library
Ferris State University
1201 S. State St.
Big Rapids, MI 49307-2747
Phone: (616) 592-3602
Great Lakes Patent and Trademark Center
Detroit Public Library
5201 Woodward Ave.
Detroit, MI 48202
Phone: (313) 833-3379

Minnesota
Minneapolis Public Library & Information Center
300 Nicollet Ave.
Minneapolis, MN 55401-1992
Phone: (612) 630-6120

Mississippi
Mississippi Library Commission
1221 Ellis Ave.
P.O. Box 10700
Jackson, MS 29289-0700
Phone: (601) 359-1036

Missouri
Linda Hall Library
5109 Cherry St.
Kansas City, MO 64110
Phone: (816) 363-4600
St. Louis Public Library
1301 Olive St.
St. Louis, MO 63103

Phone: (314) 241-2288 ext. 390

Montana
Montana Tech of the University of Montana Library
   Butte, MT 59701
   Phone: (406) 496-4281

Nebraska
Engineering Library
   Nebraska Hall
   Second Floor West
   University of Nebraska-Lincoln
   Lincoln, NE 68583-0717
   Phone: (402) 472-3411

Nevada
University Library
   University of Nevada-Reno
   Reno, NV 89557-0044
   Phone: (702) 784-6500 ext. 257

New Hampshire
New Hampshire State Library
   20 Park St.
   Concord, NH 03301-6314
   Phone: (603) 271-2239

New Jersey
Newark Public Library
   5 Washington St.
   P.O. Box 630
   Newark, NJ 07101-0630
   Phone: (973) 733-7779
Library of Science and Medicine
   Rutgers University
   New Brunswick, NJ 08903
   Phone: (732) 445-2895

New Mexico
Centennial Science and Engineering Library
   The University of New Mexico
   Albuquerque, NM 87131
   Phone: (505) 277-4412

New York
New York State Library

Science, Industry and Business Library
Cultural Education Center
Albany, NY 12230
Phone: (518) 474-5355
Buffalo and Erie County Public Library
Lafayette Square
Buffalo, NY 14203
Phone: (716) 858-7101
Science, Industry and Business Library
New York Public Library
188 Madison Ave.
New York, NY 10016
Phone: (212) 592-7000
Engineering Library
State University of New York
Stony Brook, NY 11794-3300
Phone: (516) 632-7148

North Carolina
D.H. Hill Library
North Carolina State University
Campus Box 7111
Raleigh, NC 27695-7111
Phone: (919) 515-2935

North Dakota
Chester Fritz Library
University of North Dakota
P.O. Box 9000
Grand Forks, ND 58202-9000
Phone: (701) 777-4888

Ohio
Akron-Summit County Public Library
55 S. Main St.
Akron, OH 44326-0001
Phone: (330) 643-9075
The Public Library of Cincinnati and Hamilton County
800 Vine St.
Library Square
Cincinnati, OH 45202-2071
Phone: (513) 369-6971
Cleveland Public Library
325 Superior Ave.
Cleveland, OH 44114-1271
Phone: (216) 623-2870

Ohio State University Libraries
   1858 Neil Avenue Mall
   Columbus, OH 43210-1286
   Phone: (614) 292-6175
Toledo/Lucas County Public Library
   325 N. Michigan St.
   Toledo, OH 43624-1614
   Phone: (419) 259-5212

Oklahoma
Oklahoma State University
   Stillwater, OK 74078-0375
   Phone: (405) 744-7086

Oregon
Paul L. Boley Law Library
   Lewis & Clark Law School
   Northwestern School of Law
   10015 S.W. Terwillinger Blvd.
   Portland, OR 97219
   Phone: (503) 768-6786

Pennsylvania
The Free Library of Philadelphia
   1901 Vine St.
   Philadelphia, PA 19103-1189
   Phone: (215) 686-5331
The Carnegie Library of Pittsburgh
   4400 Forbes Ave.
   Pittsburgh, PA 15213-4080
   Phone: (412) 622-3138
Fred Lewis Pattee Library—C207
   Pennsylvania State University
   505 Pattee Library
   University Park, PA 16802
   Phone: (814) 865-4861

Rhode Island
Providence Public Library
   225 Washington St.
   Providence, RI 02903
   Phone: (401) 455-8027

South Carolina
R.M. Cooper Library
   Clemson University

Clemson, SC 29634-3001
Phone: (864) 656-3024

South Dakota
Devereaux Library
  South Dakota School of Mines and Technology
  501 E. Saint Joseph St.
  Rapid City, SD 57701-3995
  Phone: (605) 394-1275

Tennessee
Memphis & Shelby County Public Library, and Information Center
  1850 Peabody Ave.
  Memphis, TN 38104
  Phone: (901) 725-8877
Stevenson Science and Engineering Library
  Vanderbilt University
  Suite 300
  Stevenson Center
  419 Twenty-first Ave. South
  Nashville, TN 37240
  Phone: (615) 322-2717

Texas
McKinney Engineering Library
  Cockrell Hall
  The University of Texas at Austin
  Austin, TX 78713
  Phone: (512) 495-4500
Sterling C. Evans Library
  Texas A&M University
  College Station, TX 77843-5000
  Phone: (409) 845-3826
Dallas Public Library
  1515 Young St.
  Dallas, TX 75201
  Phone: (214) 670-1468
South Central Intellectual Property Partnership at Rice University (SCIPPR)
  Fondren Library
  Rice University MS-220
  P.O. Box 1892
  Houston, TX 77251-1892
  Phone: (713) 285-5196
Texas Tech University Library
  Government Documents
  Eighteenth and Boston Ave.

Lubbock, TX 79409-0002
Phone: (806) 742-2282

Utah
Marriott Library
    University of Utah
    Salt Lake City, UT 84112
    Phone: (801) 581-8394

Vermont
Bailey/Howe Library
    University of Vermont
    Burlington, VT 05405
    Phone: (802) 656-2542

Virginia
James Branch Cabell Library
    Virginia Commonwealth University
    Academic Campus
    901 Park Ave.
    Richmond, VA 23284-2033
    Phone: (804) 828-1104

Washington
Engineering Library
    Engineering Library Building
    Box 352170
    University of Washington
    Seattle, WA 98195
    Phone: (206) 543-0740

West Virginia
Evansdale Library
    West Virginia University
    P.O. Box 6105
    Morgantown, WV 26506-6105
    Phone: (304) 293-2510 ext. 5113

Wisconsin
Kurt F. Wendt Library
    University of Wisconsin-Madison
    215 N. Randall Ave.
    Madison, WI 53706
    Phone: (608) 262-6845
Milwaukee Public Library
    814 W. Wisconsin Ave.

Milwaukee, WI 53233-2389
Phone: (414) 286-3051

Wyoming
Natrona County Public Library
307 E. Second St.
Casper, WY 82601
Phone: (307) 237-4935

Societies and Organizations

American Antiquarian Society
185 Salisbury St.
Worcester, MA 01609-1634
American Photographic Historical Society (APHS)
1150 Avenue of the Americas
New York, NY 10036
Phone: (212) 575-0483
American Society of Camera Collectors (ASCC)
4918 Alcove Ave.
North Hollywood, CA 91607
Phone: (818) 769-9160
Daguerreian Society
3045 W. Liberty Ave., Suite 7
Pittsburgh, PA 15216-2460
Phone: (412) 343-5525
International Kodak Historical Society
P.O. Box 21
Flourtown, PA 19031
Phone: (215) 233-2032
International Photographic Historical Organization (INPHO)
P.O. Box 16074
San Francisco, CA 94116
Phone: (415) 681-4356
Library of Congress
Local History and Genealogy Reading Room
Thomas Jefferson Bldg.
Room LJ20
10 First St., S.E.
Washington, DC 20540-5554
National Stereoscopic Association (NSA)
P.O. Box 14801
Columbus, OH 43214
Photographic Historical Society
P.O. Box 39563
Rochester, NY 14604

Stereo Photographers Collectors & Enthusiasts Club (SPCEC)
P.O. Box 2368
Culver City, CA 90231

Suppliers

The companies listed below sell materials for the long-term storage and preservation of photographs including boxes, folders, protective sleeves and albums. They also furnish catalogs free of charge.

Conservation Materials Ltd.
  1165 Marietta Way
  P.O. Box 2884
  Sparks, NV 89431
Conservation Resources
  8000-H Forbes Place
  Springfield, VA 22151
  Phone: (800) 634-6932
Gaylord Bros.
  P.O. Box 4901
  Syracuse, NY 13221-4901
  Phone: (800) 448-6160
Hollinger
  P.O. Box 6185
  Arlington, VA 22206
  Phone: (800) 634-0491
Light Impressions
  439 Monroe Ave.
  P.O. Box 940
  Rochester, NY 14603-0940
  Phone: (800) 828-6216
University Products
  517 Main St.
  P.O. Box 101
  Holyoke, MA 01041-0101
  Phone: (800) 762-1165

Conference Lectures

Tapes can be ordered from Repeat Performance, 2911 Crabapple Lane, Hobart, IN 46342, (219) 465-1234, Wcb sitc: http://www.repeatperform ance.com.

Barton, Noel R. "Photograph History and Analysis" SLC-128

Barton, Noel R. "Using Photography in Your Family History Research" SLC-182

Davis, Grant. "How to Obtain Pictures and Use Them to Produce Audio-Visual History" SLC-252

Jiloty, Richards, Bob McKeever, Terry Deglau. "Copying of Photographs: Electronically and Traditionally" FGS; "In Your Ancestor's Image" RNY-44

Kemp, Leatrice. "Dating Your Photographs," "In Your Ancestor's Image" FGS RNY-131

Lener, DeWayne. "Using Photography for Genealogy" Gentech, February 11 and 12, 1994, Dallas, Texas

Miller, Ilene. "Bring Your Family to Life with Photos and Computers" FGS/SGS-September 20-23, 1995, Seattle, Washington, SW111

Miskin, David. "Identifying, Preserving, and Restoring Your Old Photographs" VT 03-AB 2 tapes. New England Regional Conference, Portland, ME–October 22-25, 1998. 98-15; 98-10

Web Sites of Interest

Internet Source

Ancestors Found

http://www.geocities.com/Heartland/Prairie/6248/ancestors/found.html

Help for identifying photographs or items that individuals would like to return to the right family.

Civil War Family Photographs

http://members.tripod.com/~cwphotos/

Site for sharing your photographs of Civil War participants.

Collected Visions

http://cvisions.cat.nyu.edu/mantle/info.html

Submit images to an archive of family photos and write an essay to accompany them.

Daguerreian Society

http://www.daguerre.org

On-line exhibits of daguerreotypes and useful links.

George Eastman House

http://www.eastman.org

Features a timeline of photographic history and access to database of photographers.

Nebraska Gen Web Ancestors Lost and Found

http://www.rootsweb.com/~neresour/ancestors/index.html

Listings just for Nebraska.

Wallace Library Guides

http://wally.rit.edu/pubs/guides/photobio.html

Features bibliographies for nineteenth-century photographic processes.

Magazines and Catalogs To Help You Date Costume and Interior Photos

American Girl 1920-1979
American Home 1928-1978
Brides 1933-present
Cosmopolitan 1886-present
Designer and the Woman's Magazine 1894-1926?
Essence 1970-present
Frank Leslie's Ladies Journal 1871-1881
Glamour 1903-present
Godey's Lady's Book 1830-1898
Good Housekeeping 1885-present
Harper's Bazaar 1867-present
Ladie's Home Journal 1883-present
Mademoiselle 1935-present
McCall's 1876-present
Modern Bride 1950-present
The New Peterson Magazine 1842-1898
Redbook 1903-present
Seventeen 1942-present
Town & Country 1846-present
Vogue 1892-present
Woman's Wear Daily 1910-present
Woman's Day 1937-present
Woman's Home Companion 1873-1957
Working Woman 1976-present
Young Miss 1953-present

Store Catalogs
Jordan Marsh
Marshall Field
Montgomery Wards
Sears, Roebuck and Co.

Printed Source

Worksheets

Sources

Following are blank copies of forms used to help focus your research when studying cased images (page 19), prints (pages 23–30) and negatives (page 30).

These forms are copyright 2000 by Maureen Taylor, but you are free to photocopy them for your personal use. No use in a printed work is permitted without permission.

KEY TO WORKSHEETS

Approximate date of negative: Based on the type of negative and the support material.

Case manufacturer: Name of manufacturer.

Coloring details: Outline what parts of the image are colored.

Condition: Assign a value (poor, fair, good, excellent) to the condition of the image, negative or cased image. Describe any damage.

Costume description: Using the charts in chapter eight, Identifying Costume, briefly describe what the individuals are wearing.

Costume time frame: Assign dates to the costume styles.

Date print from negative made: When was a print made from the negative.

Description of case design: Identify the key elements of the design.

Hinges: Describe the type of hinges and clasp used on the case.

Identifying marks: Make note on your worksheet of business cards, patent notices, etc., found on the back of the image.

Mounted: Yes or no.

Original or copy print: Date of copy print if known.

Owner's name and address: Be as complete as possible. Previous owners can be recorded on the back of the work sheet.

Photographer's dates of operation: Dates when the photographer was in business.

Photographer's imprint: Record type of imprint and the exact way it appears on the image.

Photographer's name: Include this if known. This is different from photographer's imprint.

Props/background: Describe the types of props and background used.

Size of case: Dimensions in inches.

Support material for negatives: Glass, paper or film.

Title/Subject/Caption: Copy information as it appears on the image. Place handwritten captions in quotation marks. Titles you assign should be placed in brackets. Include life dates for the subjects if known.

Type of case: Wood, cardboard, leather or union case.

Type of image: Daguerreotype, ambrotype or tintype, etc.

Type of mount: What the photograph is attached to, such as glass, board or metal.

Type of negative: Glass, paper, nitrate or safety film.

Whereabouts of negative: Complete information on the owner of the negative if known.

CASED IMAGE

Attach photocopy of image	Title/Subject/Caption
	Identifying marks
	Photographer's name
	Coloring details
	Costume description
	Other

Owner's name	
Address	
Telephone number	
Condition	
Type of image	
Type of case	
Size	
Hinges	
Case Manufacturer	
Description of case design	
Dates of operation	
Props/background	
Costume time frame	

PRINTS

Attach photocopy of image	Title/Subject/Caption
	Identifying marks
	Photographer's name
	Coloring details
	Costume description
	Other

Owner's name	
Address	
Telephone number	
Condition	
Type of image	
Size	
Mounted	
Thickness	
Type of mount	
Original or copy print	
Date of copy print	
Photographer's imprint	
Dates of operation	
Props/background	
Costume time frame	
Whereabouts of negative	

PRINTS (GROUP PORTRAITS)

Attach photocopy of image	Title/Subject/Caption
	Identifying marks
	Photographer's name
	Coloring details
	Costume description
	Other

Owner's name	
Address	
Telephone number	
Condition	
Type of image	
Size	
Mounted	
Thickness	
Type of mount	
Original or copy print	
Date of copy print	
Photographer's imprint	
Dates of operation	
Props/background	
Costume time frame	
Whereabouts of negative	

NEGATIVES

	Title/Subject/Caption
Attach photocopy of image	Identifying marks
	Photographer's name
	Coloring/touch up details
	Costume description
	Other

Owner's name	
Address	
Telephone number	
Condition	
Type of negative	
Size	
Support material	
Approximate date	
Photographer's imprint	
Dates of operation	
Props/background	
Costume time frame	
Date print from negative made	

Bibliography

Printed Source

Baldwin, G. *Looking at Photographs: Guide to Technical Terms.* Santa Monica, Calif.: J. Paul Getty Museum in Association with British Museum Press, 1991.

Capa, Cornell, ed. *International Center of Photography Encyclopedia of Photography.* New York: Crown Publishers, Inc., 1994.

Coe, Brian, and Mark Haworth-Booth. *A Guide to Early Photographic Processes.* London: The Victoria and Albert Museum in Association with Hurtwood Press, 1983.

Crawford, W. *The Keepers of Light, History and Working Guide to Early Photographic Processes.* Dobbs Ferry, N.Y.: Morgan and Morgan, 1979.

Dunkelman, Mark. "An Interview with Michael J. Winey, Curator at the U.S. Army Military History Institute," *Military Images* (November-December, 1993): 9-16.

Dunkelman, Mark, and Michael Winey. "Precious Shadows: The Importance of Photographs to Civil War Soldiers, as Revealed by a Typical Union Regiment," *Military Images* (July-August 1994): 6-13.

Eskind, Andrew H. and Greg Drake, eds. *Index to American Photographic Collections: Compiled at the International Museum of Photography at George Eastman House.* 3d enlarged edition. New York: G.K. Hall & Co., 1996.

Foresta, Merry A. *American Photographs: The First Century.* Washington, DC: Smithsonian Institution Press, 1997.

Gernsheim, Helmut, and Alison Gernsheim. *The History of Photography From the Camera Obscura to the Beginning of the Modern Era.* New York: McGraw-Hill, 1969.

Johnson, William S. *International Photography Index.* Annual. 1979, 1980, 1981. Boston: G.K. Hall, 1983-.

Johnson, William S. *Nineteenth Century Photography: An Annotated Bibliography, 1839-1879.* Boston: G.K. Hall & Co., 1990.

Leggett, M.D., comp. *Subject-Matter Index of Patents for Inventions Issued by the United States Patent Office from 1790 to 1873.* Washington, DC: Government Printing Office, 1874. Reprint 3 vols. New York: Arno Press, 1976.

McDarrah, Gloria S., Fred W. McDarrah and Timothy S. McDarrah. *The Photography Encyclopedia.* New York: Schirmer Books, 1999.

Morris, Andrew J. "Photography and Genealogy." http://www.genealogy.org/~ajmorris/photo/pg.htm

Newhall, Beaumont. *The History of Photography.* New York: The Museum of Modern Art, 1982.

Palmquist, Peter E., ed. *Photographers: A Sourcebook for Historical Research.* Brownsville, Calif.: Carl Mautz Publishing, 1991.

Public Record Office. *An Introduction to 19th and Early 20th Century*

Photographic Processes. Public Record Office Series: Introduction to Archival Materials. London: Public Record Office, 1996.

Roosens, Laurent, and Luc Salu. *History of Photography: A Bibliography of Books.* 2 vols. New York: Mansell, 1989.

Sandweiss, Martha A., ed. *Photography in Nineteenth-Century America.* Fort Worth, Tex.: Amon Carter Museum, 1991.

Sennet, Robert S. *Photography and Photographers to 1900: An Annotated Bibliography.* Garland Reference Library of the Humanities. New York: Garland Publishing, 1985.

Taft, Robert. *Photography and the American Scene: A Social History, 1839-1889* (1938, reprint) New York: Dover Publications, 1964.

Walrath, Paul. "Photography and Kodak: A Path to the Past," *FGS Forum* 9 (1997): 4-7.

Welling, William. *Photography in America: The Formative Years, 1839-1900.* New York: Thomas Y. Crowell Company, 1978.

Backdrops

Neal, Avon. "Folk Art Fantasies: Photographers' Backdrops," *Afterimage* 24 (April/May 1997): 13-18.

Color

Dmitri, Ivan. *Kodachrome and How to Use It.* New York: Simon and Schuster, 1940

Henisch, Heniz, and Bridget A. Henisch. *The Painted Photograph, 1839-1914: Origins, Techniques, Aspirations.* University Park, Pa.: Pennsylvania State University Press, 1996.

Sipley, Louis Walton. *A Half Century of Color.* New York: Macmillan Co., 1951.

Wilhelm, Henry. *The Permanence and Care of Color Photographs: Traditional and Digital Color Prints, Color Negatives, Slides and Motion Pictures.* Grinnell, Iowa: Preservation Publishing Company, 1993.

Wood, John. *The Art of the Autochrome.* Iowa City, Iowa: University of Iowa Press, 1993.

Costume

Batterberry, Michael and Ariane. *Mirror Mirror: A Social History of Fashion.* New York: Holt, Rinehart & Winston, 1977.

Blum, Stella. *Everyday Fashions of the Thirties as Pictured in Sears Catalogs.* New York: Dover Publications, 1986.

———. *Everyday Fashions of the Twenties as Pictured in Sears and Other Catalogs.* New York: Dover Publications, 1981.

———. *Victorian Fashions & Costumes from Harper's Bazaar, 1867-1898.* New York: Dover Publications, 1974.

Corson, Richard. *Fashions in Hair: The First Five Thousand Years.* New York: Hastings House Publishers, 1965.

Cumming, Valerie. *Gloves*. The Costume Accessories Series, Dr. Aileen Ribeiro. London: B.T. Batsford, Ltd., 1982.

Cunningham, Patricia A., and Susan Voso Lab, eds. *Dress in American Culture*. Bowling Green, Ohio: Bowling Green State University, 1993.

Cunnington, Phillis. *Costume of Household Servants From the Middle Ages to 1900*. London: Adam and Charles Black, 1974.

Danky, James P. *Women's Periodicals and Newspapers From the 18th Century to 1981*. Boston: G.K. Hall, 1982.

Espinosa, Carmen. *Shawls, Crinolines, Filigree: The Dress and Adornment of the Women of New Mexico, 1739-1900*. El Paso,: Texas Western Press at The University of Texas at El Paso, 1970.

Ewing, Elizabeth. *Dress and Undress: A History of Women's Underwear*. New York: Drama Book Specialists, 1978.

Fales, Martha Gandy. *Jewelry in America 1600-1900*. Woodbridge, Suffolk, U.K.: Antique Collector's Club, 1995.

Foster, Vanda. *Bags & Purses*. The Costume Accessories Series, General Editor, Dr. Aileen Ribeiro. London: B.T. Batsford, 1982.

Gottlieb, Robert, and Frank Maresca, eds. *A Certain Style: The Art of the Plastic Handbag, 1949-59*. New York: Alfred A. Knopf, 1988.

McClellan, Elizabeth. *Historic Dress in America, 1607-1870*. New York: Arno Press, 1977.

Melinkoff, Ellen. *What We Wore: An Offbeat Social History of Women's Clothing, 1950–1980*. New York: W. Morrow, 1984.

Olian, Joanne. *Everyday Fashions 1909-1920 as Pictured in Sears Catalogs*. New York: Dover, 1995.

———. *Everyday Fashions of the Forties as Pictured in Sears Catalogs*. New York: Dover, 1992.

Peacock, John. *Men's Fashion: The Complete Sourcebook*. London: Thames and Hudson, 1996.

———. *20th Century Fashion: The Complete Sourcebook*. London: Thames and Hudson, 1993.

Probert, Christina. *Hats in Vogue Since 1910*. New York: Abbeville Press, 1981.

Rose, Clare. *Children's Clothes Since 1750*. London: B.T. Batsford, 1989.

Severa, Joan L. *Dressed for the Photographer: Ordinary Americans and Fashion, 1840–1900*. Kent, Ohio: Kent State University Press, 1995.

Shep, R.L. *Civil War Gentlemen: 1860's Apparel Arts & Uniforms*. Mendocino, Calif.: R.L. Shep, 1994.

Swan, Jane. *Shoes*. The Costume Accessories Series, General Editor, Dr Aileen Ribeiro. London: B.T. Batsford, 1982.

Taylor, Lou. *Mourning Dress: A Costume and Social History*. London: George Allen and Wunwin, 1983.

Thieme, Otto Charles, et al. *With Grace & Favor: Victorian & Edwardian Fashion in America*. Cincinnati: Cincinnati Art Museum, 1993.

Trasko, Mary. *Heavenly Soles: Extraordinary Twentieth-Century Shoes*. New York: Abbeville Press, 1989.

Daguerreotypes

Barger, Susan M., and William B. White. *The Daguerreotype: Nineteenth Century Technology and Modern Science.* Washington, DC: Smithsonian Institution Press, 1991.

Berg, Paul. *Nineteenth Century Photographic Cases and Wall Frames.* Huntington Beach, Calif.: Huntington Valley Press, 1995.

The Daguerreian Annual. Pittsburgh: The Daguerreian Society.

Field, Richard S., and Robin Jaffee Frank. *American Daguerreotypes From the Matthew R. Isenburg Collection.* New Haven, Conn.: Yale University, 1990.

Foresta, Merry A., and John Wood. *Secrets of the Dark Chamber: The Art of the American Daguerreotype.* Washington, DC: National Museum of American Art, Smithsonian Institution Press, 1995.

Krainik, Clifford, and Michele Krainik with Carl Walvoord. *Union Cases: A Collector's Guide to the Art of America's First Plastic.* Grantsburg, Wisc.: Centennial Photo Services, 1988.

Newhall, Beaumont. *The Daguerreotype in America.* New York: Duell, Sloan & Pearce, 1961. Reprint New York: Dover Publications, Inc. 1976.

Rinhart, Floyd, and Marion Rinhart. *American Case Art.* New York: A.S. Barnes and Company, 1969.

———. *American Daguerrean Art.* New York: Clarkson N. Potter, 1967.

———. *The American Daguerreotype.* Athens, Ga.: University of Georgia Press, 1981.

Rudisill, Richard. *Mirror Image: The Influence of the Daguerreotype on American Society.* Albuquerque: University of New Mexico Press, 1971.

Wood, John. ed.. *America and the Daguerreotype.* Iowa City: University of Iowa Press, 1991.

———. *The Scenic Daguerreotype: Romanticism & Early Photography.* Iowa City: University of Iowa Press, 1995.

Family Reunions

Beasley, Donna. "Family Reunion Planning Tips," *American Visions* 13 (April-May 1998): S36.

Giles, Dari. "Getting Together With Family: The Key to Having a Great Family Reunion Lies in the Planning," *Black Enterprise* 27 (February 1997): 213-214.

Negatives

Patti, Tony. "Historically Speaking. Discovery of the Collodion Process in Photography," *PSA Journal* 60 (January 1994): 7.

Postmortem

Burns, Stanley B. *Sleeping Beauty: Memorial Photography in America.* Altadena, Calif.: Twelvetrees Press, 1990.

Meinwald, Dan. "Memento Mori: Death and Photography in Nineteenth Century America." http://cmp1.ucr.edu/terminals/memento_mori

Ruby, Jay. *Secure the Shadow: Death and Photography in America*. Cambridge, Mass.: MIT Press, 1995.

Prints
Darrah, William. *Cartes de Visite in Nineteenth Century Photography*. Gettysburg, Pa: the author, 1981.

Gagel, Diane VanSkiver. "Card and Paper Photographs, 1854-1900," *Ancestry* 15 (September/October 1997): 13-17.

Reilly, James M. *Care and Identification of 19th Century Photographic Prints*. Rochester: Kodak Publications, 1986.

Stereographs
Bennett, Mary, and Paul C. Juhl. *Iowa Stereographs: Three-Dimensional Visions of the Past*. Iowa City: University of Iowa Press, 1997.

Darrah, William C. *Stereoviews: A History of Stereographs in America and Their Collection*. Gettysburg, Pa.: Times and News Publishing Co., 1964.

Darrah, William C. *The World of Stereographs*. Gettysburg, Pa: the author, 1977.

Waldsmith, John. *Stereo Views, An Illustrated History and Price Guide*. Radnor, Pa.: Wallace-Homestead Book Company, 1991.

Tintypes
Burns, Stanley B., M.D. *Forgotten Marriage: The Painted Tintype & The Decorative Frame 1860-1910: A Lost Chapter in American Portraiture*. New York: The Burns Collection, Ltd., 1995.

Lindgren, C.E. "Caring for Tintypes & Creating New Ones," *PSA Journal* 59 (January 1993): 17-18.

SOURCES

Sources of Information About Photographers

This checklist includes material that a researcher should be able to locate. For additional listings and material on foreign photographers see Richard Rudisill's essay in *Photographers: A Sourcebook for Historical Research* (Brownsville, Calif.: Carl Mautz Publishing, 1991).

Printed Source

General

Craig, John S. *Craig's Daguerreian Registry, Vol 1-3*. Torrington, Conn.: John S. Craig, 1994, 1996.

Darrah, William. *Stereoviews*. Gettysburg, Pa.: Times and News Publishing Co., 1961.

Drake, Greg. "Nineteenth-Century Photography in the Upper Connecticut Valley: An Annotated Checklist," *Dartmouth College Library Bulletin 25* (April 1985): 72-91.

Fleming, Paula Richardson, and Judith Luskey. *The North American Indians in Early Photographs*. New York: Harper & Row, Publishers, 1986.

Kelbaugh, Ross J. *Directory of Civil War Photographers*. Vol. I, Maryland, Delaware, Washington, DC, Northern Virginia. Baltimore, Md.: Historic Graphics, 1990. Vol. II : Pennsylvania, New Jersey.

————. *Directory of Civil War Photographers*. Baltimore, Md.: Historic Graphics, 1991.

Mautz, Carl. *Checklist of Western Photographers: A Reference Workbook*. Mendocino, Calif.: Black Bear Press, 1986.

Moutoussany-Ashe, Jeanne. *Viewfinders: Black Women Photographers*. New York: Dodd, Mead & Company, 1986.

Robinson, William F. *A Certain Slant of Light: The First Hundred Years of New England Photography*. Boston: New York Graphic Society, 1980.

Rosenblum, Naomi. *A History of Women Photographers*. New York: Abbeville Press, Inc. 1994.

Smith, James H., & Co. *A List of All the Professional Photographers in the United States and Canada*. Chicago: James H. Smith & Co., 1893.

Treadwell, T.K. Tex, and William C. Darrah. *Stereophotographers Index*. Columbus, Ohio: National Stereoscopic Association, 1993.

Union Guide to Photograph Collections in the Pacific Northwest. Portland, Ore.: Oregon Historical Society, 1978.

Willis-Thomas, Deborah. *An Illustrated Bio-Bibliography of Black Photographers 1940-1988*. New York: Garland Publishing, Inc. 1988.

————. *Black Photographers, 1840-1940: Illustrated Bio-Bibliography*. New York: Garland Publishing, Inc., 1985.

Witham, George F., comp. *Catalogue of Civil War Photographers: A Listing of Civil War Photographers' Imprints*. Portland, Ore.: Privately Published, 1988.

Alabama

McLaurin, Melton A., and Michael V. Thomason. *The Image of Progress: Alabama Photographs, 1872-1917*. Tuscaloosa, Ala.: University of Alabama Press, 1980.

Alaska

"Biographies of Pioneers," *Pathfinder* 1 (December 1919): 8-16.

Mattison, David. "Photo Nuggets—Klondike Photographers," *Beaver* 77 (October/November 1997): 33-39.

Arizona

Daniels, David. "Photography's Wet-Plate Interlude in Arizona Territory: 1864-1880," *The Journal of Arizona History* 9 (Winter 1968): 171-194.

Hooper, Bruce. "Camera on the Mogollon Rim: Nineteenth Century Photography in Flagstaff, Arizona Territory, 1867-1916," *History of Photography* 12 (April-June 1988): 93-100.

———. "Chronology of Commercial Photography and Stereography in Arizona Territory, in Arizona Territorial Stereography-Part IV," *Stereo World* 13 (September/October 1986): 29, 48.

———. "Stoneman Lake: One of Arizona's Early Tourist Attractions Stereographed by D.F Mitchell and W.H. Williscraft, 1875-1883," *Stereo World* 12 (September/October 1985): 37-40, 47.

Rowe, Jeremy. *Photographers in Arizona 1850-1920: A History & Directory*. Nevada City, Calif.: Carl Mautz Publishing, 1995.

Spude, Robert L. "Shadow Catchers: A Portrait of Arizona's Pioneer Photographers, 1863-1893," *Journal of Arizona History* 30 (1989): 233-250.

California

Caddick, James L. *Directory of Photographers in the San Francisco Bay Area to 1900*. San Francisco: Privately compiled, 1985.

Callarman, Barbara Dye. *Photographers of Nineteenth Century Los Angeles County*. Los Angeles: Hacienda Gateway Press, 1993.

Latour, Ira H., ed. *Silver Shadows: A Directory and History of Early Photography in Chico and Twelve Counties of Northern California*. Chico, Calif.: Chico Museum Association, 1993.

Palmquist, Peter E. *Shadowcasters: A Directory of Women in California Photography Before 1901*. Arcata, Calif.: Peter E. Palmquist, 1990.

———. *Shadowcasters II: A Directory of Women in California Photography, 1900-1920*. Arcata, Calif.: Peter E. Palmquist, 1991.

Palmquist, Peter E., with Lincoln Kilian. *The Photographers of the Humboldt Bay Region*. Vols. 1-7. Arcata, Calif.: Peter E. Palmquist, 1987.

Colorado

Harber, Opal. "A Few Early Photographers of Colorado," *Colorado Magazine* 33 (October 1956): 284-295.

———. *Photographers and the Colorado Scene 1853-1900*. Denver: Western History Department, Denver Public Library, 1961.

————. *Photographers and the Colorado Scene 1901-1941*. Paonia, Colo.: Opal Harber, 1977.

Connecticut

Fuller, Sue Elizabeth. "Checklist of Connecticut Photographers by Town: 1839-1889" and "Alphabetical Index of Connecticut Photographers: 1839-1889," *The Connecticut Historical Society Bulletin* 47 (Winter 1982): 117-154, 155-163.

Robinson, William F. *The Connecticut Yankee & the Camera: 1839-1889*. Hartford: The Connecticut Historical Society, 1983.

Delaware

Williams, Jon M. "Daguerreotypists, Ambrotypists, and Photographers in Wilmington, Delaware, 1842-1859." *Delaware History* 18 (1979): 180-193.

District of Columbia

Buseyu, Samuel C. "Early History of Daguerreotypy in the City of Washington," *Records of the Columbia Historical Society*. 3 (1900): 81-95.

Florida

Rinhart, Floyd, and Marion Rinhart. *Victorian Florida*. Atlanta: Peachtree Publishers Ltd., 1988.

————. *Victorian Florida: America's Last Frontier*. Atlanta: Peachtree Publishers Ltd., 1986.

Hawaii

Abramson, Joan. *Photographers of Old Hawaii*. Honolulu: Island Heritage, 1976.

Idaho

Hart, Arthur A. *Camera Eye on Idaho: Pioneer Photography, 1863-1913*. Caldwell, Idaho: The Caxton Printers, Ltd., 1990.

Illinois

Czach, Marie. *A Directory of Early Illinois Photographers*. Macomb: Western Illinois University, 1977.

Kansas

Taft, Robert. "A Photographic History of Early Kansas," *Kansas Historical Quarterly* 3 (February 1934): 3-14.

Louisiana

Smith, Margaret Denton. "Checklist of Photographers Working in New Orleans, 1840-1865," *Louisiana History* 20 (1979): 393-430.

Smith, Margaret Denton, and Mary Louise Tucker. *Photography in New Orleans: The Early Years, 1840-1865*. Baton Rouge: Louisiana State University Press, 1982.

Maine
Darrah, William C., comp. *A Checklist of Maine Photographers Who Issued Stereographs—A Special Supplement to the Maine Historical Society News-Letter*, May 1967.

Maryland
Kelbaugh, Ross J. "Dawn of the Daguerrean Era in Baltimore, 1839-1849," *Maryland Historical Magazine* 84 (Summer 1989): 101-118.
———. *Directory of Maryland Photographers, 1839-1900*. Baltimore: Historic Graphics, 1988.
———. *Supplemental Directory of Baltimore Daguerreotypists*. Baltimore: Historic Graphics, 1989.
Warren, Mame, and Marion E. Warren. *Maryland Time Exposures, 1840-1940*. Baltimore: Johns Hopkins University Press, 1984.

Massachusetts
Steele, Chris, and Ron Polito. *A Directory of Massachusetts Photographers 1839-1900*. Camden, Me.: Picton Press, 1993.

Michigan
Welch, Richard W. *Sun Pictures in Kalamazoo: A History of Daguerreotype Photography in Kalamazoo County, Michigan 1839-1860*. Kalamazoo, Mich.: Kalamazoo Public Museum, 1974.

Minnesota
Baker, Tracey. "Nineteenth-Century Minnesota Women Photographers," *Journal of the West* 28 (1989): 15-23.
Wilson, Bonnie G. "Working the Light: Nineteenth-Century Professional Photographers in Minnesota," *Minnesota History* 52 (1990): 42-60.

Missouri
Van Ravenswaay, Charles. "The Pioneer Photographers of St. Louis," *Bulletin of the Missouri Historical Society* 10 (October 1953): 49-71.

Montana
Gray, John S. "Itinerant Frontier Photographers and Images Lost, Strayed or Stolen," *Montana—The Magazine of History* 28 (April 1978): 2-15.
Morrow, Delores J. "Female Photographers on the Frontier: Montana's Lady Photographic Artists, 1860-1900," *Montana: The Magazine of Western History* 32 (Summer 1982): 76-84.

Nebraska

Kennedy, Martha H. "Nebraska's Women Photographers," *Nebraska History* 72 (1991): 62-77.

New Hampshire

Drake, Greg. "Nineteenth Century Photography in the Upper Connecticut Valley: An Annotated Checklist," *Dartmouth College Library* 25 (April 1985): 92-100.

New Jersey

Moss, George H., Jr. *Double Exposure: Early Stereographic Views of Historic Monmouth County, New Jersey and Their Relationship to Pioneer Photography*. Sea Bright, N.J.: Ploughshare Press, 1971.

New Mexico

Coke, Van Deren. *Photography in New Mexico: From the Daguerreotype to the Present*. Albuquerque: University of New Mexico Press, 1979.

Rudisill, Richard. *Photographers of the New Mexico Territory, 1854-1912*. Santa Fe: University Printing Plant, 1973.

New York

Bannon, Anthony, et al. *The Photo-Pictorialists of Buffalo*. Buffalo: Media Study, 1981.

Christopher, A.J. "Early Village Photographers," *Balwinsville Messenger*, July 24, 1974.

Fordyce, Robert Penn, comp. *Stereo Photography in Rochester, New York up to 1900: A Record of the Photographers and Publishers of Stereographs*. Rochester: Privately Published, 1975.

Gabriel, Cleota Reed. "A Bibliography of Early Syracuse Photographers," *Photograhica: A Publication of the Photograhic Historical Society of New York* 13 (October 1981): 12-13.

Vetter, Jacob C. "Early Photographers: Their Parlors and Galleries," *Chemung County Historical Journal* (June 1961): 853-860.

North Dakota

Vyzralek, Frank E. "Dakota Images: Early Photographers and Photography in North Dakota, 1853-1925," *North Dakota History: Journal of the Northern Plains* 57 (Summer 1990): 24-37.

Ohio

Fullerton, Richard D., comp. *99 Years of Dayton Photographers*. Dayton, Ohio: Richard D. Fullerton, 1982.

Gagel, Diane VanSkiver. *Photography in Ohio 1839-1900: A History & Directory*. Nevada City, Calif.: Carl Mautz Publishing, 1998.

Oregon

Culp, Edwin D. "Oregon Postcards," *Oregon Historical Quarterly* 66 (December 1965): 303-330.

Goodman, Theodosia Teel. "Early Oregon Daguerreotypers and Portrait Photographers," *Oregon Historical Quaterly* 49 (March 1948): 30-49.

Robinson, Thomas. *Oregon Photographers: Biographical History and Directory, 1852-1917.* Portland, Ore.: Thomas Robinson, 1992.

Toedtemeier, Terry. "Oregon Photography: The First Fifty Years," *Oregon Historical Quarterly* 94 (1993): 36-76.

Pennsylvania

Finkel, Kenneth. *Nineteenth-Century Photography in Philadelphia: 250 Historic Prints from the Library Company of Philadelphia.* New York: Dover Publications, Inc., 1980.

Heisey, M. Luther. "The Art of Photography in Lancaster," *Papers of the Lancaster County Historical Society* 51 (1947): 93-114.

Panzer, Mary. *Philadelphia Naturalistic Photography 1865-1906.* New Haven, Conn.: Yale University Art Gallery, 1982.

Patterson, Rosemary A. "Early Photography in Lancaster," *Journal of the Lancaster County Historical Society* 87 (1983): 34-52.

Powell, Pamela C. *Reflected Light: A Century of Photography in Chester County.* West Chester, Pa.: Chester County Historical Society, 1988.

Weprich, Thomas M. "Pioneer Photographers in Pittsburgh, Pennsylvania," *Pennsylvania History* 64 (Spring 1997): 193-203.

Rhode Island

Taylor, Maureen. "Nature Caught at the Twinkling of an Eye: The Daguerreotype in Providence," *Rhode Island History* 42 (November 1983): 109-121.

———. "Never Give Up; It is Better to Hope than Once to Despair: Providence, Rhode Island, and the Daguerreotype," *The Daguerreian Annual* (1995): 127-134.

Tennessee

Reynolds, Ann, and John Compton. "Nashville Photographers, 1853-1935," recorded in *Nashville–A Visual Record by the City's Early Photographers.* Nashville, Tenn.: Metropolitan Historical Commission, 1980, pp. 29-30.

Texas

Haynes, David. *Catching Shadows: A Directory of Nineteenth-Century Texas Photographers.* Austin: Texas State Historical Association, 1993.

Utah

Carter, Kate B., comp. *Early Pioneer Photographers.* Salt Lake City: Daughters of Utah Pioneers, 1975.

————. *The Story of an Old Album.* Salt Lake City: Daughters of Utah Pioneers, 1947.

Wadsworth, Nelson. *Through Camera Eyes.* Salt Lake City: Brigham Young University Press, 1975.

————. "Zion's Cameramen: Early Photographers of Utah and the Mormons," *Utah Historical Quarterly* 40 (Winter 1972): 24-54.

Virginia

Ginsberg, Louis. *Photographers in Virginia 1839-1900: A Check List.* Petersburg, Va.: Louis Ginsberg, 1986.

Washington

Jones, Gordon. "Short Biographies of Photographers Who Help Record the Maritime History of the Pacific Northwest," *Puget Sound Maritime Historical Association Newsletter Supplement* (November 1966).

Wisconsin

Adams-Graf, John, comp. "A Directory of Green Bay Photographers: 1847-1890," *Voyageur: Northeast Wisconsin Historical Review* 12 (1995): 2-7.

Index

More Great Books Full of Great Ideas!

Unpuzzling Your Past: A Basic Guide to Genealogy—140,000 copies sold! Make uncovering your roots easy with this complete genealogical research guide. You'll find everything you need—handy forms, sample letters and worksheets, census extraction forms, a comprehensive resource section, bibliographies and case studies. Plus, updated information on researching courthouse records, federal government resources and computers on genealogy.
#70301/$14.99/180 pages/paperback

The Unpuzzling Your Past Workbook: Essential Forms and Letters for All Genealogists—Now unpuzzling your past is easier than ever using forty-two genealogical forms designed to make organizing, searching, record-keeping and presenting information effortless.
#70327/$15.99/320 pages/paperback

The Handybook for Genealogists, Ninth Edition—More than 750,000 copies sold! Since 1947, the Handybook has proven itself as the most popular and comprehensive research aid available for tracking down major state and county records essential to genealogists. Save countless hours of your research time by consulting its up-to-date listings of archives, genealogical libraries and societies. State profiles cover history and list sources for maps, census and church records. The county profiles tell you where to find custody records, property records and key addresses. Color maps are included of each state and their counties.
#70411/$34.99/380 pages/60 color maps/ hardcover

First Steps in Genealogy—If you're just stepping into the fascinating field of genealogy, this book will get you off to a successful start. Desmond Walls Allen, a recognized genealogical expert, will teach you step-by-step how to define your goals and uncover facts about the people behind the names and dates. Learn to organize your research with pedigree charts, group sheets and filing systems. Discover what sources are available for research, starting with your family scrapbook or attic. Also included are sample forms, a resource directory and glossary.
#70400/$14.99/128 pages/paperback

Organizing Your Family History Search—Few hobbies generate more paperwork than genealogy. Sharon DeBartolo Carmack shows you how to successfully tackle the arduous process of organizing family research, from filing piles of paper to streamlining the process as a whole. With her flexible filing system and special research notebook, she reveals how you can free up time, conduct better research and become a more effective genealogist.
#70425/$16.99/176 pages/paperback

The Genealogist's Companion & Sourcebook—115,000 copies sold! Uncover promising new sources of information about your family history. This hands-on guide shows you how to get past common obstacles—such as lost public records—and discover new information sources like church and funeral home records, government documents, newspapers and maps.
#70235/$16.99/256 pages/paperback

A Genealogist's Guide to Discovering Your Female Ancestors—Discover special strategies for overcoming the unique challenges of tracing female genealogy. This comprehensive guide shows you methods for determining maiden names and parental lineage: how to access official documents; plus where to find information unique to women of ethnic origins. Also included is a glossary of terms specific to female genealogy, a detailed bibliography with more than 200 resources, plus and extensive source checklist.
#70386/$17.99/144 pages/paperback

A Genealogist's Guide to Discovering Your Italian Ancestors—This easy-to-use reference guides you step-by-step through researching your Italian ancestors—as far back as the 1700s! You'll learn how to find—and read—Italian vital records; write letters requesting data from Italian officials; and use American records like census and naturalization records, and family letteres and church records. You'll also find information on how to read foreign handwriting, and much more. *#70370/$16.99/128 pages/ 42 b&w illus./paperback*

How to Tape Instant Oral Biographies, Second Edition—With fun interviewing techniques and exercises, family members of all ages will learn how to spark memories, recall treasured stories, and relate old family anecdotes, sayings, recipes and more. Comes complete with blank family history sheets and work pages.
#70448/$12.99/144 pages/paperback

How to Write the Story of Your Life—This friendly guide makes memoir writing an enjoyable undertaking—even if you're a nonwriter. Five hundred "memory sparkers" will help you recall forgotten events in each stage of your life and 100 topic ideas help add variety to your story. Includes excerpts from actual memoirs and plenty of encouragement to keep you moving your story towards completion.
#10132/$14.99/230 pages/paperback

Writing Family Histories and Memoirs—Your family history and personal stories are too vital to lose. Turn them into a lively record for the next generation with this handy writing reference. You'll find helpful how-to advice on working from memories and interviewing family members, using public records, writing and publishing.
#70295/$14.99/272 pages/paperback

Writing Life Stories—Creative writing instructor Bill Roorbach explains how you can turn your life's untold stories into vivid personal essays and riveting memoirs. His advice and exercises will open up your memories, help you shape life events into plot lines and craft finely-wrought stories worthy of publication.
#48035/$17.99/224 pages/hardcover

Reaching Back—Record life's most meaningful moments to share with future generations. This easy-to-use keepsake edition includes space for family stories, photos, heirlooms, family trees, and helps you research and record you family's unique history.
#70360/$14.99/160 pages/paperback

Family History Logbook—Weave your personal history into the colorful web of national events. You'll find an extensive list of historical events spanning the years 1900 to 2000, along with a special section to record your own milestones.
#70345/$16.99/224 pages/paperback

The Everyday Life Series

You've tracked down vital statistics for your great great grandparents, but do you know what their everyday lives were like? These titles will give you a vivid and detailed picture of life in their own time. Learn what your relatives likely wore, what they ate, and how they talked. Social and religious customs, major occupations and family life are all covered. These "slice-of-life" facts will readily round out any family history.

The Writer's Guide to Everyday Life...

... from Prohibition to World War II *#10450/$18.99/272 pages/hardcover*

... in Renaissance England *#10484/$18.99/272 pages/hardcover*

... in Regency and Victorian England *#10545/$18.99/240 pages/hardcover*

... in the 1800's *#10353/$18.99/320 pages/hardcover*

... in the Wild West *#10600/$18.99/336 pages/hardcover*

... in Colonial America *#10640/$14.99/288 pages/paperback*

... During the Civil War *#10635/$16.99/288 pages/paperback*

Creating Family Newsletters—This idea-packed book shows you how to write and design family newsletters that will bring "mail box cheer" to your friends and relatives the world over. More than 100 full-color examples—from hand-crafted to computer generated—offer great ideas for creating your own unique newsletters for every occasion. *#10558/$19.99/120 color illus./128 pages/paperback*

Scrapbook Storytelling, Step by Step—Go beyond typical scrapbooking techniques! Here is how to recall your favorite family stories and combine them with cherished photos, collages and illustrations to create unique booklets, albums, gift items and more. *#70450/$19.99/120 color illus./128 pages/paperback*

Publishing Your Family History on the Internet—With this first-ever guide, even if you're a beginning computer user, you can design and publish your own genealogical Web sites. Learn how to display your family history data—including pictures, sounds and video—onto the Web. *#70447/$19.99/320 pages/140 b&w illus./paperback*

The Internet for Genealogists, Fourth Edition—This completely revised and updated guide to the latest genealogy Web sites will give you quick access to the resources you need. Includes more than 200 addresses to genealogy sites, libraries, catalogs, maps, gazetteers, bookstores, on-line databases and living persons directories. *#70415/$16.99/192 pages/paperback*

Charting Your Family History: The Legacy Family Tree Software Solution—Now you can organize your genealogical records with ease, thanks to the Legacy Family Tree software on CD-ROM—the most comprehensive and easy-to-use genealogy software on the market today. Legacy allows unlimited data input, viewing of up to seven Family or Pedigree views at one time, over twenty customized reports plus the linking of pictures and sounds to any member of your family tree. System requirements: IBM 486 or faster compatibles, minimum 8MB memory, 20MB hard drive space, Windows 3.1 or Windows 95, VGA or higher. *#70420/$49.95/270 page book with PC compatible CD-ROM*

Families Writing—Here is a book that details why and how to record words that go straight to the heart—the simple, vital words that will speak to those you care most about and to their descendants many years from now. *10294/$14.99/198 pages/paperback*

Turning Life Into Fiction—Learn how to turn your life, those of friends and family members, and newspaper accounts into fictional novels and short stories. Through insightful commentary and hands-on exercises, you'll hone the essential skills of creating fiction from journal entries, identifying the memories ripest for development, ethically fictionalizing other people's stories, gaining distance from personal experience and much more. *#48000/$17.99/208 pages*

How to Have a 48-Hour Day—Get more done and have more fun as you double what you can do in a day! Aslett reveals reasons to be more productive everywhere—and what "production" actually is. You'll learn how to keep accomplishing despite setbacks, ways to boost effectiveness, the things that help your productivity and much more. *#70339/$12.99/160 pages/120 illus./paperback*

Make Your House Do the Housework, Revised Edition—Take advantage of new work-saving products, materials and approaches to make your house keep itself in order. You'll discover page after page of practical, environmentally-friendly new ideas and methods for minimizing home cleaning and maintenance. *#70293/$14.99/208 pages/215 b&w illus./paperback*

Stephanie Culp's 12-Month Organizer and Project Planner—The projects you're burning to start or yearning to finish will zoom toward accomplishment by using these forms, "To-Do" lists, checklists and calendars. Culp helps you break any project into manageable segments, set deadlines, establish plans and follow them—step by attainable step. *#70274/$12.99/192 pages/paperback*

Don Aslett's Clutter-Free! Finally and Forever—Free yourself of unnecessary stuff that chokes your home and clogs your life! If you feel owned by your belongings, you'll discover incredible excuses people use for allowing clutter, how to beat the "no-time" excuse, how to determine what's junk, how to prevent recluttering and much more! *#70306/$12.99/224 pages/50 illus./paperback*

Confessions of a Happily Organized Family—Learn how to make your mornings peaceful, chores more fun and mealtime more relaxing by getting the whole family organized. *#70338/$12.99/240 pages/paperback*

Clutter's Last Stand—You think you're organized, yet closets bulge around you. Get out of clutter denial with loads of practical advice. *#01122/$12.99/280 pages/paperback*

Office Clutter Cure—Discover how to clear out office clutter—overflowing "in" boxes, messy desks and bulging filing cabinets. Don Aslett offers a cure for

every kind of office clutter that hinders productivity—even mental clutter like gossip and office politics. *#70296/$10.99/ 192 pages/175 b&w illus./paperback*

It's Here . . . Somewhere—Need help getting and keeping your busy household in order? This book provides step-by-step instruction on how to get more places out of spaces with a room-by-room approach

to organization. *#10214/$10.99/192 pages/50 b&w illus./paperback*

How to Get Organized When You Don't Have the Time—You keep meaning to organize the closet and clean out the garage, but who has the time? Culp combines proven time-management principles with practical ideas to help you clean up key trouble spots in a hurry.

#01354/$14.99/216 pages/paperback

How to Conquer Clutter—Think of this book as a "first aide guide" for when you wake up and find that clutter has once again taken over every inch of available space you have. You'll get insightful hints from A to Z on how to free yourself from clutter's grasp. *#10119/$12.99/184 pages/paperback*